P9-CBF-522

Beyond the Image

THE HISTORY OF THE CHURCH
THROUGH ICONOGRAPHY

✝ ✝ ✝

Saint Nicholas Antiochian Orthodox Church
GRAND RAPIDS, MICHIGAN

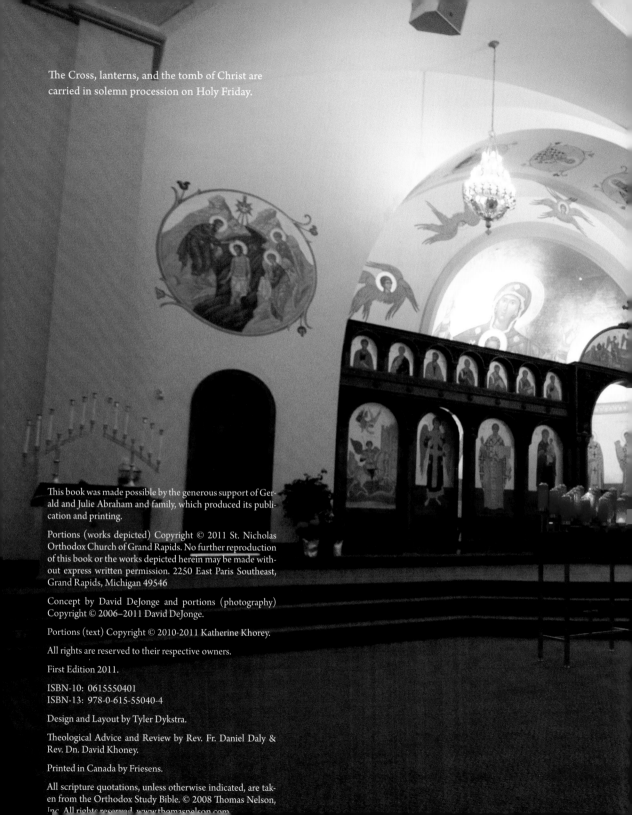

The Cross, lanterns, and the tomb of Christ are carried in solemn procession on Holy Friday.

This book was made possible by the generous support of Gerald and Julie Abraham and family, which produced its publication and printing.

First Edition 2011.

ISBN-10: 0615550401
ISBN-13: 978-0-615-55040-4

Design and Layout by Tyler Dykstra.

Theological Advice and Review by Rev. Fr. Daniel Daly & Rev. Dn. David Khoney.

Printed in Canada by Friesens.

James Abraham
1921-2009

Georgette Helen Abraham
1923-1989

From your Children and their Families

Contents

left   A portion of the iconostasis, depicting several saints and Apostles

below   Paints and mixing cups, used for touchups and for painting the scenery around the saints, rest high above the nave floor

Introduction

ON ICONOGRAPHY

ORTHODOX CHRISTIANS BELIEVE THAT GOD BECAME MAN through the Incarnation of Jesus Christ. Is this a truth we can see with our own eyes? That is, how can we come to know Christ and His Church better, particularly through the use of our sense of sight? If God made man "in His image and likeness," and Christ is God, do we merely contemplate these matters in the abstract, or can we "come and see?"

Images have had a vital place in the Christian experience since the Ascension of Christ. The images depicted on the walls of the Roman catacombs, where the first faithful secretly gathered, are some of the first examples of the use of images in Christian life. Even today, new examples of these ancient images continue to be discovered as technology makes such discoveries possible.

These early images drew upon both the unique symbols and signs devised by Christians and those recognized by their contemporaries. Images served not only to remind and instruct the faithful of the articles of their faith, but also as objects of veneration, attesting to a faith that proclaimed the presence of Christ and the reality of the Kingdom of Heaven. In a hostile environment, the images made by the early Christians kept their articles of faith in some degree of seclusion from the authorities; often early Christian art would be purposely depicted in a manner that would make understanding it difficult for those not initiated in the faith.

A few centuries later, when the Roman Empire stopped persecuting Christians and when the Christian faith was even embraced by the emperors themselves, Christian art began to naturally flourish. Secrecy was no longer necessary. While the Church grew, the centrality of images in the Christian religion remained.

Over the next centuries Christian art, mainly in the West, developed in more literal and secular directions, while in the East

the style—or rather the theology—of that form of imagery we know as iconography remained essentially unchanged, even to the present day. The earliest known icons possessed today, those which survived the centuries of *iconoclasm*—the violent conflict over the rightness of imagery in Christianity, which was resolved in support of icons at the Seventh Ecumenical Council in the ninth century—date back as far as the fourth century. These early icons resemble those being made in the traditional fashion today: all contemporary iconographers base their own work directly on that which preceded them. These links of precedence run all the way back to the catacombs.

Tracing its roots to Christ and His Apostles, the Orthodox Church values, and always has valued, the use of images in worship and prayer. It defines the purpose and significance of the *icon* (Greek for *image*) very specifically.

At the heart of Orthodox Christian belief lies the Incarnation of Christ. For Orthodox Christians, God's act of taking on our human nature, while remaining divine without confusion or division, repairs the previously-severed connection between God and Man, and makes our salvation possible in the Resurrection.

Indeed, every aspect of Orthodox tradition reflects a facet of the Incarnation. Services, prayers, scriptures, and other writings express as much through words. Icons, defined by the Church as images of persons or events sacred to Orthodoxy painted according to the precedent of Church tradition, serve as objects of prayer and instruction in both Orthodox parish churches and private homes. Icons not only depict the Incarnation through particular images, but also by the nature of the medium itself. Just as God became a tangible and comprehensible man, allowing us access to His unknowable divinity, so an icon—like Jesus Christ Himself—consists essentially of a divine concept otherwise beyond our perception, yet now portrayed and made present in physical and solid matter. An icon thus makes that which it depicts perceivable, understandable, and accessible, and therefore testifies to the Incarnate reality of the God-man Himself.

Just as Jesus Christ did not lose His divinity upon taking flesh, so icons, while physical objects, maintain a vital spiritual and sacred aspect. Thus, the artistic traditions of iconogra-

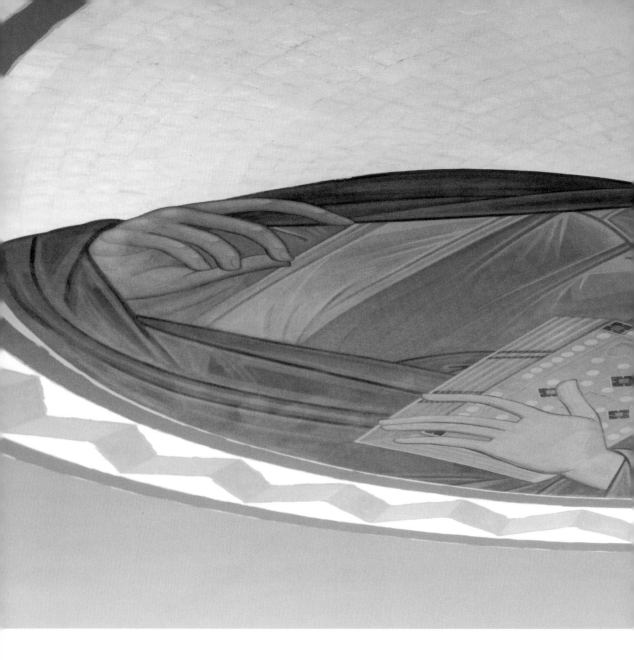

phy do not reflect the physical laws of gravity, proportion, or perspective. Rather, icons portray the aspects and beauty of the world *beyond* the physical one, and are sometimes called "windows to Heaven." This divine quality gives us a real view to the icons' glorified subjects, and makes possible our prayer, not *to* the icons themselves, but *through* them. While an icon is, therefore, an image made by humans from earthly materials, it nonetheless bears a divine character through which we may apprehend, approach, and perhaps even encounter holiness.

Iconographers must be spiritually prepared to pursue their work. An iconographer undergoes a period of prayer and fasting as part of his or her painting process, and in the work itself makes use of specific colors, symbols, and facial features whose set meaning and significance in an icon have been passed down since the Church's beginning. These details will be discussed in greater detail throughout this book as they apply to each icon in the sanctuary of St. Nicholas Orthodox Church, as will the significance of particular icons' specific placement within the temple or sanctuary at St. Nicholas.

Finally, while the icons at St. Nicholas preserve all these traditions and fulfill all these purposes—as do all true icons—they also possess unique characteristics of their own. As icons are human creations, they reflect ourselves as fundamentally identical, yet still unique creatures, as living icons of God.

The icons at St. Nicholas also tell the story of God revealing Himself and saving His people, from Creation until today. They express the history of our salvation and our faith in images, as "theology in color." The icons depict Christ, His Mother, the prophets, the apostles, and the saints, all the way to saints of the present day. As windows to Heaven, they do more than illustrate historical events and figures. They portray the life of Christ, His Church and His saints in a way that is made real to those who see through the icons their own path to salvation, in living color.

This path begins with God before our knowledge of time, and travels from the historical revelation to Abraham and his descendants, up to the present day and beyond. Today, we do not need to keep the faith presented in the Church's icons secret. In fact, there is every need to proclaim it. Through a fuller and deeper understanding and contemplation of the icons, one may see, and come to know, Christ and His Church.

10-11 The iconographers begin applying the gold leaf surrounding the dome Pantocrator icon

12 *(Above)* Inspecting the paint and gold leaf *(Right)* Father Theodore designs letter templates as he discusses the project with one of his assistants

12-13 Father Theodore works on the scenery surrounding the icon of Saint John the Evangelist (p. 92)

14-15 Father Theodore and his handiwork in the dome of St. Nicholas Church

15 Sitting at the pinnacle of a network of scaffolding, Father Theodore takes a break and surveys some of his icons of the Old Testament prophets

The Iconographer

FATHER THEODORE KOUFOS

T HE ICONS PORTRAYED IN THIS BOOK WERE MADE BY THE hand of Father Theodore Koufos.

Father Theodore was born in Boston in 1940 and attended high school there. He earned his B. A. in Anthropology at the University of Buffalo, and then took a teaching assistantship at the University of South Florida. While there, he also earned his Masters of Fine Arts in painting at Hillsborough Community College in Tampa.

Father Theodore received his seminary training at Holy Trinity Seminary in New York. There, in what he calls a "fluke," he encountered two "masters" of iconography, Archimandrite Cyprian (now deceased) and Archbishop Alypy of Chicago, who were both teaching at the seminary while he was a student. Father Theodore was always interested in iconography, and now that he was able to study with both masters in the seminary's icon studio, he began his work in the Byzantine tradition of iconography.

Father Theodore credits his work with Archimandrite Cyprian and Archbishop Alypy at Holy Trinity as sealing his interest in iconography. Ever since that time, throughout his priesthood, he has been painting (or, as it is sometimes called, "writing") icons. He has become known for developing an aesthetic that involves elements of both Slavic and Greco-Byzantine traditions of iconography: Father Theodore has adopted both the "poeticness" of the Slavic style and the "impact" of the Byzantine style. He "[likes] to emphasize detail" in his icons, "so the closer you get to the work, the more you see." His "coloration," or *palette*, is "flowerlike; while the subject is intense and deep, I like the coloring to be very alluring, comforting, joyful."

Currently based in Toronto, Father Theodore has designed and produced iconography in a wide variety of churches in many

locations throughout North America, including in the sanctuary of St. John the Baptist Cathedral in Washington DC.

Realizing that "every architectural setting sets the mood" of a given parish church, he adapted his work to the space of St. Nicholas Orthodox Church accordingly. Thus, Father Theodore arranged certain icons according to the "standard placing" in a typical Orthodox church, but also allowed for specific variations for St. Nicholas. The sanctuary at St. Nicholas is so vast and "airy," and the "dome is so large," for example, that Father Theodore concluded that "covering every inch" with icons and decoration—as might be done in a smaller, more intimate setting— would be "overwhelming." Thus, he deliberately left white space throughout the sanctuary, "to keep it airy," and "translucent," and to "allow eyes to float peacefully from one icon to the next."

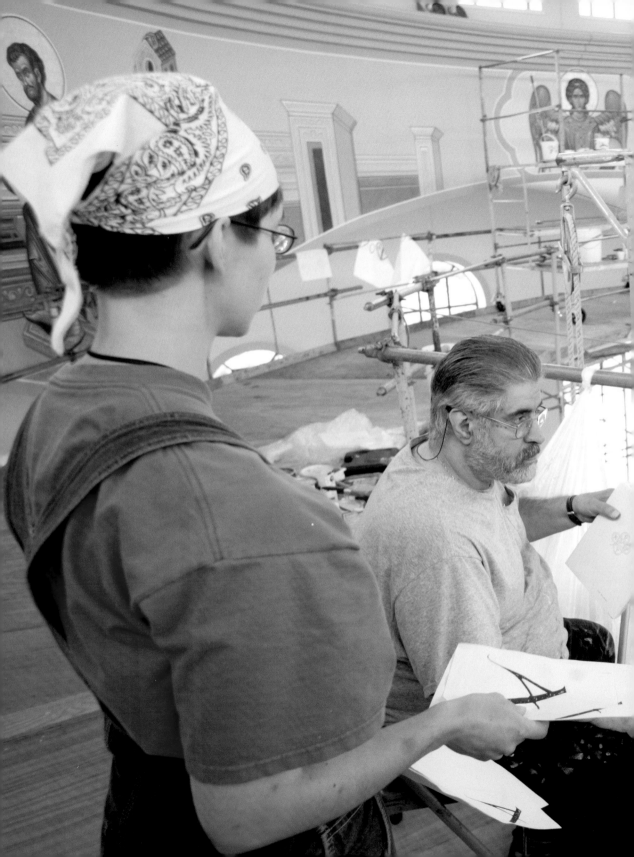

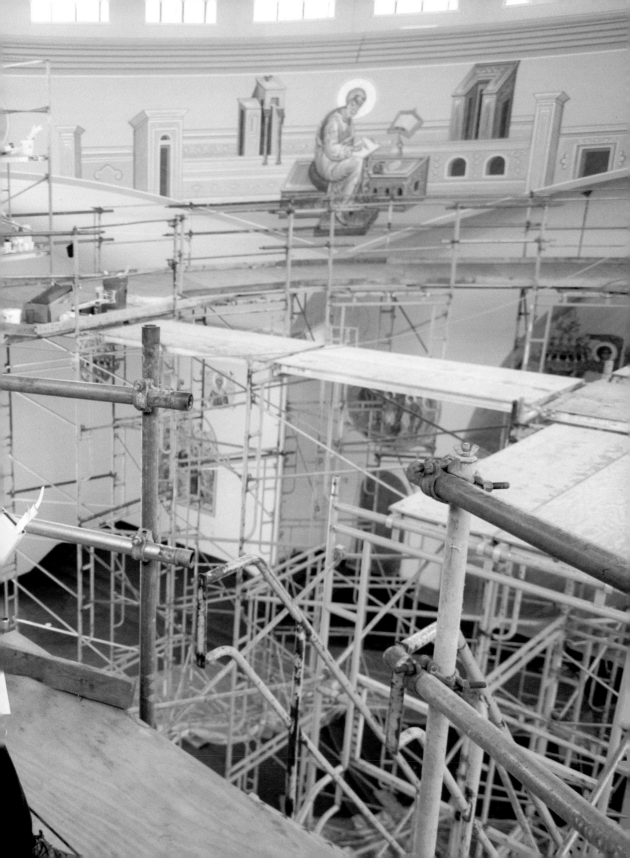

22 An archangel holds a medallion depicting Emmanuel, representing Christ's eternal, timeless nature; the medallion itself represents the scales of judgment

22-23 The icon of Christ Pantocrator looks down from the completed dome above the nave

Ages of Ages

ABOVE SPACE & TIME

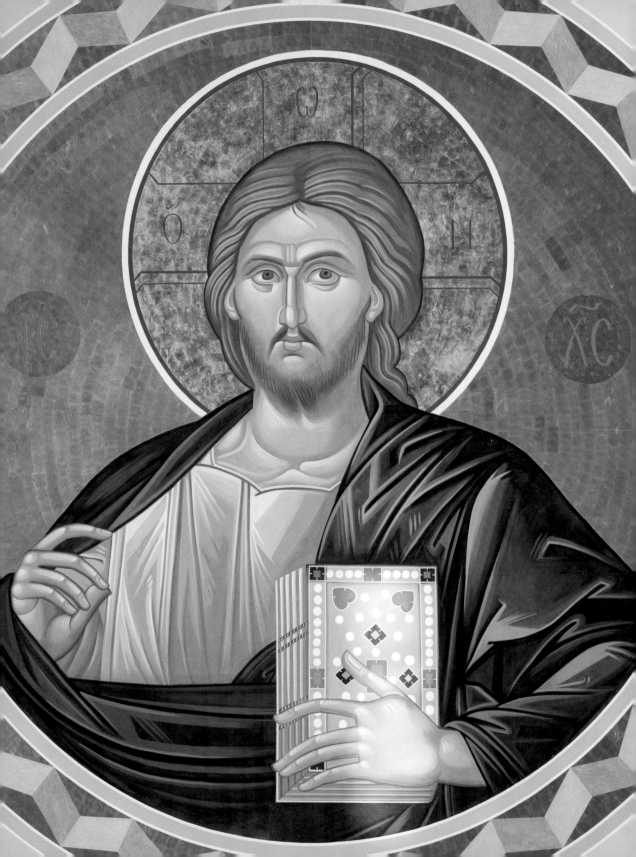

Jesus Christ, the Pantocrator

THE LARGE ICON WHICH FILLS THE DOME depicts Jesus Christ as *Pantocrator*, or the Master of all that is seen and unseen, the Alpha and the Omega, the beginning and the end. This icon will always—as is appropriate to the authority it represents—be located in a church's highest dome or *cupola*. The placement of Christ as Pantocrator at the highest central point of the church building represents His place as the center of all things in Church life.

The subjects of all icons resemble one another in their non-naturalistic portrayal (as the icon's focus is on spiritual realities, rather than physical appearances, so human features appear distorted to reflect their actual glorification), but the individuals portrayed are nonetheless recognizable, from icon to icon, as uniquely themselves. Christ Himself is perhaps the easiest to identify in this way.

The Pantocrator icon contains several additional symbols that hold true in every icon of Jesus. Its gold background represents eternal life, and holiness beyond all earthly context. Jesus is identified by the Greek initials for His name, *IC XC* for *Iēsoûs Xristós* (Greek for *Jesus Christ*), and on the gold *nimbus* around his head, the Greek phrase *O ŌN*, "the Existing One" or "the One Who Is," after God's declaration "I AM." His clothing is colored to represent His dual nature: the red for His divinity, and the blue for His humanity.

Our Lord is also identified by the inscriptions on each icon. The declaration "I AM" expresses the encompassing and incomprehensible nature of God's being. Jesus' right hand is raised in a Byzantine blessing: His paired fingers representing His divine and human natures, and His other two fingers, placed with His thumb, represent the Holy Trinity. In other versions, the book Jesus holds is open to a scripture passage ("I am the Light of the world," or "He who follows Me walks not in darkness but in light") that emphasizes His power as a Redeemer and Teacher (Jn. 8:12). At St. Nicholas, however, Jesus' closed book—the Book of Life—represents both the finality of the Last Judgment and the fact that the rendering of this Judgment is, for each of us, both unmade and unknown.

The dominant placement of the Pantocrator icon high above the church reminds both that Christ is not only the Alpha, but also the Omega, the one who begotten before all time, gives life to all, rules over all, and finally judges all in a Kingdom to come. No other icon has such preëminence in the church.

The Holy Trinity (The Hospitality of Abraham)

THE ICON ABOVE THE CENTRAL DOORS, or Holy Doors, of the iconostasis bears two meanings.

The first depicts a scene from the Bible. The image of three angels grouped around a food-laden table is understood to illustrate the story of the Hospitality of Abraham (Gen. 18:1-8). Here Abraham had just been told by God that he and his wife, Sarah, though beyond childbearing age, were to be blessed with a son. Shortly thereafter, Abraham greeted three men—messengers from Heaven, but also guests in their own right and entitled to good treatment—who appeared on his doorstep. Abraham did all he could to make his holy visitors comfortable, and with Sarah's help served them from the best provisions he could offer. The guests confirmed Abraham's blessing. Consistent with a Scriptural interpretation, they are portrayed as angels.

Second, while the icon does show the three messengers seated at Abraham's table,

icons like this one have come to be understood throughout Church history to be representations of the Holy Trinity, present even in the Old Testament covenant God made with Abraham.

It is not necessary, though, to identify each angel in the icon as the Father, the Son, and the Holy Spirit. Different versions of the icon may reconcile the question by different means—in some, one angel is clearly identifiable as the Son, and in others, which emphasize the unity of the three Persons of the Trinity, all three angels are identical.

Other icons, like this one, make the angels both united and unique. The eyes of each angel are focused on the companion sitting to his right. The lines of their gazes form a triangle suggesting that, despite their separateness , they are united in one existence. Their placement above the Holy Doors, through which Holy Communion is brought out during the Divine Liturgy, furthers their connection to God's becoming incarnate for

our salvation and being present today in the Eucharist. The angels, unified around the feast, are partaking of Holy Communion themselves.

Also, while the three are otherwise identical to one another, they are clothed in different colors: one in red, one in blue, and one in green. These colors all have divine significance: red for active power and sacrifice for God's purpose, blue to the contemplative depths and mysteries of God's love and presence, and green for the peace and regeneration brought forth in communion between God and ourselves . The three colors, in both their meanings and appearance, complement and balance one another. Here balanced are the opposite tones of red-orange and blue, and midpoint in green: here is present the God who smote Sodom and Gomorrah, the God willing to have mercy on either city for the sake of one just citizen, and the God who delivered a child and heir to an aging couple long after they had accepted this was impossible; and, while we may not be able to pinpoint which figure is which, here are represented the Father, the Son, and the Holy Spirit.

The Archangels and Bodiless Powers

AN ANGEL IS A MESSENGER OF GOD, AND a being which has stood before God and praised Him from a time before human comprehension. We cannot fully grasp what an angel's exact nature is, but we can understand an angel's function on earth. In icons, angels—especially the high-ranking Archangels—are depicted in an earthly form. All the Archangels are dressed as humans, in clothing accented with gold, the color of holiness and Heaven.

In many Orthodox churches, icons of the Archangels will be located on the side doors, or deacon's doors, of the iconostasis. Just as a deacon acts as a messenger during the Liturgy, bringing the Gospel and the Mysteries of the altar out to the assembled faithful and leading the faithful in prayer, so have the Archangels brought God's works and messages from Heaven to the world. At St. Nicholas, three Archangels also appear around the outer ring of the dome, giving signs of Jesus' coming.

The icon of the Archangel Michael is located on the south deacon's door. Michael is the warrior of God, and in any given instance of heavenly warfare is likely present fighting for Him. In icons, Michael can always be identified by his soldier's attire, his armor, and the sword

FEAST DAYS
November 8 and September 6

FEAST DAYS
March 26 and July 13

TROPARION

Tone 4. O Commanders of the Heavenly Host, we the unworthy beseech you, that through your entreaties you will fortify us, guarding us in the shelter of the wings of your ethereal glory, even as we fervently bow before you crying: "Deliver us from all danger, as Commanders of the Powers on high!"

he wields. Also, Michael is frequently clothed in some shade of red: note his orange-hued cloak here. The color red can symbolize power, war, blood, and sacrifice: all appropriate to the angel who is engaged in warfare.

Not only is the icon of Gabriel placed on the opposite deacon's door, but Gabriel himself, as the key liaison between God's work and human comprehension of it, is clothed in a deacon's vestments. Here his vestments are green, a color which contrasts to red in its connection to peaceful renewal and the mediating power of the Holy Spirit through the sacraments. Gabriel also carries a reed, which shows that he bears messages in peace.

The Archangels beneath the dome are not named. Unlike Michael and Gabriel they do not serve a specific function; instead they represent the purpose of all angels. They display signs of Jesus' coming to earth, glorifying Him as He comes. One angel, in purple with a red mantle, holds a medallion bearing an icon of the child Jesus (p. 22). The other two, in green and in red, hold medallions inscribed with the Greek letter *X*, the first initial of *Christ* in Greek. All the angels' arms are raised or open to the Pantocrator icon. Like the other saints depicted in the dome, they praise the Son of God and make clear His presence.

The icons of the Seraphim, which attend the large *Platytera* icon of the Theotokos and Christ in the apse of the church (p. 66), do not express as particular a message as the icons of the Holy Trinity and the Archangels. While the latter icons show their subjects in some detail, the Seraphim are simply portrayed as winged and haloed human faces.

But this simple depiction explains the angels' nature as far as we can understand it. The Seraphim have faces of men because an angel communicates God's acts and intentions on earth, while their gold nimbuses show their heavenly nature and their bodiless wings, in defiance of our understanding and expectation, the mystery of that heavenly nature.

The number and color of the wings are also significant. A prayer in the Divine Liturgy refers to Seraphim and Cherubim as "six-winged," as they are described in Isaiah 6:2.

The wings are also all shaded in either purple or red, both colors denoting majesty and power. The detail of the Seraphim icons, as well as their overall design, shows the function, power, and high heavenly standing of the angels.

PROPHET ELISHA PROPHET JEREMIAH PROPHET AARON

JONAH PROPHET

prophet zechariah

prophet obadiah

prophet ezekiel

prophet zachariah prophet hosea prophet zephaniah prophet amos prophet solomon prophet eliah prophet

ĪC ΧС

Ō Ω Ν

The Prophets

THE OLD TESTAMENT

THE ICONS OF SIXTEEN OLD TESTAMENT prophets are arranged in a circle surrounding the Pantocrator icon. The men depicted here, through their communion with God, foresaw, foretold and laid the way not only for the birth and Resurrection of Jesus Christ in the New Testament, but also for His second coming. For this reason we know them as *prophets*.

While their circular arrangement around the Pantocrator represents the prophets' unity of purpose, each icon portrays the individual aspects of their lives and works.

The earliest prophet shown here is Moses.

32-33 The Prophets of the Old Testament, these sixteen and others, pointed the Israelite people to their coming Messiah and Christ. In the same way, the array of Old Testament Prophets direct the eye to the Pantocrator icon at the pinnacle of the dome.

FEAST DAY
September 4

TROPARION
Tone 2. As we celebrate the memory of
Thy Prophet Moses, O Lord, through
him we beseech Thee to save our souls.

Prophet Moses   *c. 1600 BC*

MOSES, AS A PROPHET, TRANSCRIBER OF HOLY
Law, and mediator between God and man, is the
earliest of the Old Testament figures to be portrayed in
the dome. Through Moses, God made Himself known
to the people of Israel. In his obedience to God and his
communication of the Law to the people, Moses laid the
foundation for our salvation through the New Covenant
made in Christ.

Scripture tells us that Moses, a child of the enslaved
Israelites, was adopted into the Egyptian royal family in
his infancy. Through his older sister's resourcefulness, his
own mother was hired as his nurse, and he knew his birth
family throughout his life.

When Moses reached adulthood, he witnessed
firsthand the injustice of the Egyptian enslavement of his
people, and having committed murder in righteous an-
ger, retreated into hiding in a nearby land, taking on the
life of a shepherd.

As Moses adapted to his new setting, the Israelites'
suffering in Egypt continued. But "their cry came up to
God because of their labors. So God heard their groan-
ing, … [and] God looked down about the children of Israel and was made known to them" (Ex. 2:23-25).

God made Himself known to the people through
Moses. Although he was at first unsure of his own ability to
carry out God's plan to free and lead the Israelites, Moses
spent the remainder of his long life revealing the wonders
of God as he freed the Israelites from Egypt, guiding his

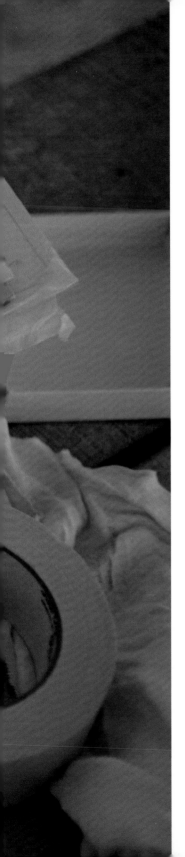

people through bouts of privation and back from periods of doubt and rebellion, and enacting God's commands regarding the rites of worship they were to follow and the rules of the society they were to form. It is through Moses that God sent the Ten Commandments, as well as the Old Law's vast catalog of other tenets, and established the tabernacle with its ark of the covenant as where God met His people, prefiguring Christ as God dwelling among the people.

Moses died, leaving a God-appointed successor, Joshua, having seen the land promised by God to the Israelites.

In his mediation between God and the Israelites, in his role in their earthly salvation, and in his compiling of the Law, which Christ would come to fulfill, Moses acts as a precursor to the Incarnate Son of God.

Moses appears twice in the iconography at St. Nicholas. He is shown in the icon of the Transfiguration (p. 102), as well as here in the dome.

The icon in the dome shows Moses not in his role as a shepherd, as he was when God first spoke to him, but elevated to a state of leadership and power. Moses' red, purple, blue, and gold attire does not represent earthly royalty, but rather his reign as the leader who brought the Israelites to fulfill God's promise. He holds his scroll firmly in both hands, presenting the Law directly to the people as God gave it to them. His scroll reads "May the heavens rejoice with him, may all the earth adore," a standard excerpt to be included in an icon of Moses, taken from the song of praise he made shortly before his death (Deut. 32:43). In this context and in this setting high in the dome, these words identify and praise God as Pantocrator.

Prophet Aaron *c. 1600 BC*

AARON, THE BROTHER OF MOSES, IS THE NEXT prophet. While God assigned the task of Israelite leadership directly to Moses, Aaron became an important leader in his own right.

At his first encounter with God, Moses expressed concern that he was not well-spoken enough to gain the peoples' trust and asked that God send someone better-suited. God reminded him that his brother Aaron was a Levite, from a priestly line, and was used to a position of authority and pastorship. God instructed Moses that Aaron would speak to the people in his place (Ex. 4:10-16). Aaron also frequently stood by Moses in the period before the Israelites left Egypt, and through him many miracles were accomplished that made their exodus possible.

Throughout the journey of the Israelites and God's guidance of them, Aaron continued as "spokesman to the people." Gradually the people established lasting places and forms of worship, and Aaron's role became that of a rabbi or priest. In this way Aaron is also a precursor to the leaders of the Church.

Aaron is recognizable a by his vestments, which resemble an Orthodox priest's vestments. Aaron's red *mitre* (hat) shows that he is a high priest. He carries his miracle-working staff and a blue vessel painted with the face of the Theotokos, the Virgin Mary. This vessel holds the holy manna, the food God provided in the desert. The vessel points to Mary as the holder of the true Manna from heaven— Christ—who we receive as divine food at the Eucharist.

FEAST DAY
Sunday of the Fathers

KONTAKION (FOR MOSES)
Tone 4. The choir of prophets rejoices with Moses and Aaron today, for the fulfillment of their prophecy is in our midst. The Cross, by which You have saved us, shines forth today. By their prayers, O Christ God, have mercy on us.

FEED DAY

FEAST DAY
August 20

TROPARION

Tone 2. You were given as a precious gift to a barren womb, and offered as a fragrant sacrifice to your Lord. You served Him in truth and righteousness; wherefore we honor you, O Samuel prophet of God, as an intercessor for our souls.

Prophet Samuel   *c. 1040 BC*

SAMUEL'S PROPHECIES WERE A DRIVING FORCE IN the era after the Israelites had settled in one land. His conception and birth, after his then-barren mother Hannah offered her sorrow to God and asked for His mercy and blessing, foreshadows the conception and birth of Jesus.

Hannah dedicated her son to God from the time of his birth. Eli, a priest who knew Samuel's parents and gave him religious instruction in his youth, was told by God that Samuel "shall walk before My Christ forever" (1 Kgd. 2:45).

Samuel fulfilled God's decree first by his birth, which foreshadows Jesus' birth. Also, Samuel always faithfully did God's will.

Like Aaron, Samuel is attired in the icon as a priest, having been dedicated to the temple as a baby. In his right hand he holds a *censer*, a vessel for the diffusing of incense, and in his left a *shofar*, or horn used to hold holy oil, representing Samuel's anointment of two kings in his lifetime.

When the Israelites had demanded a king, God, though not pleased, granted them one. Samuel found and enthroned the first king, Saul, whom God had selected. When the Israelites repented of their choice, Samuel assured them that God would forgive and provide if they remained obedient. Samuel kept advising Saul, though Saul often refused to take his advice. Samuel continued to mediate between God and king when he anointed Saul's successor, David.

Prophet David

c. 1000 BC

DAVID, WHO WAS ADVISED BY SAMUEL THROUGH-out his life, stabilized Israel and fortified it well against enemies. David is also known as the Psalmist, composing songs and poems that glorify God, describe His nature and coming, and our faith.

David's life prefigures the power, wisdom, and earthly arrival of Christ. God's choosing David as king before Saul's reign had ended mirrors Christ bringing a new order to the world. God's support of David in battle reflects Christ's power on earth. David also once danced, rejoicing and in a state of undress, before the Ark of the Covenant. This image is repeated in the New Testament when John the Baptist leapt for joy in his mother's womb when he encountered the unborn Jesus within the New Ark, the Theotokos.

David was only human and committed many sins, but he always recognized his guilt and confessed his sins before God. God said, "I will raise up your seed after you, who will come from your body, and I will prepare his kingdom. He shall build a house for My name, and I will establish his throne forever" (2 Kgd. 7:12-13). God refers not only to David's son and successor Solomon, and his building of the Temple, but also points to the "kingdom" established by Christ, who would be born of David's line.

In the icon, David wears the gold crown and his red and blue-purple robes of a king. He is also shown as a Psalmist, writing, "O Lord how great are they works, in wisdom hast thou made them all" (Ps. 103:24). His eyes are raised to the Pantocrator icon, showing his devotion to God.

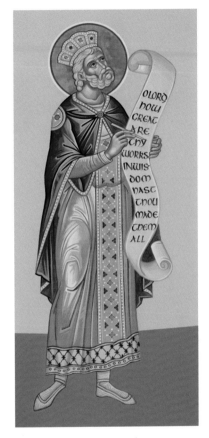

FEAST DAY
Sunday After the Nativity of Christ

TROPARION
Tone 2. Proclaim the wonder, O Joseph, to David, the ancestor of God: you saw a Virgin great with Child, you gave glory with the shepherds, you worshipped with the Magi, you received the news from the angel. Pray to Christ God to save our souls!

43

TROPARION (THE FOREFATHERS)
Tone 2. Through faith You justified the Forefathers, betrothing through them the Church of the gentiles. These saints exult in glory, for from their seed came forth a glorious fruit: She who bore You without seed. So by their prayers, O Christ God, have mercy on us!

Prophet Solomon   *c. 970 BC*

DAVID'S SON SOLOMON WAS APPOINTED BY GOD as king shortly before David died. Because "the Lord gave discernment to Solomon, exceedingly great wisdom and a heart as broad as the sand alongside the sea," Solomon's early reign was successful by earthly standards, and he performed God's work. God "was pleased" that Solomon desired only to be able to rule wisely, and promised him greater earthly success and longer life, provided Solomon "keep My commandments and My statutes Moses set before you" (3 Kgd. 3:4-13).

For a long while, Solomon did keep God's commandments, and built a temple to house the Ark of the Covenant. Significantly, the temple was decorated with holy images of Cherubim, precursors to the icons we are studying now. These were not graven idols to be worshiped, rather they were to glorify and illuminate the True God.

Unfortunately, near the end of his life Solomon briefly turned away from God, and God declared He would dissolve the kingdom in the next generation.

Solomon's renowned wisdom is immortalized in books of Scripture—Proverbs, Ecclesiastes, Song of Songs and the Wisdom of Solomon are attributed to him—and he has his place in the genealogy of Jesus.

In the icon of Solomon, the words on his scroll refer to the fruits of his wisdom: "Wisdom hath builded her house" is the start of a long metaphor on wisdom's virtues (Pr. 9). Solomon is attired like David, crowned and in red and blue, as a powerful and holy king.

Prophet Elijah

c. 875 BC

ELIJAH IS THE FIRST OF THE PROPHETS PORTRAYED here to not have been an official leader of Israel. Rather, Elijah (or in Greek, *Elias*) lived under the rule of Ahab, "who did evil before the Lord, more than all who were before him" (3 Kgd. 16:38). Through Elijah, God gave the world a voice of justice in an unjust time. But the miracles and signs worked through Elijah prefigure those Jesus worked during His life.

Leaving Israel to be humbled in a state of drought, Elijah followed God's command to sojourn by the Brook Cherith, where he was miraculously fed, like the Israelites were during their exodus from Egypt. Later, God directed Elijah to the house of a poor widow, who in reward for her hospitality and faith was told that her "bin of flour shall not be used up, and the jar of oil shall not run dry, until the day the Lord sends rain on the earth" (3 Kgd. 17:14). This miracle parallels Jesus' multiplying a small number of loaves and fishes to feed a hungry crowd. Elijah also, by the name of the Lord, restored the widow's son to life—just as Jesus was later to restore more than one child, and adult.

When he returned to Ahab, upon God's promise of rain in Israel, Elijah was made able not only to denounce the bad king but also to bring back some of those who Ahab's reign had led astray. By publicly presenting signs from God—including a mingling of fire and water that illustrates the purifying power of Baptism—Elijah brought a group of confused Israelites back to true belief. Jesus'

FEAST DAY
July 20

TROPARION
Tone 4. An angel in the flesh and the cornerstone of the prophets, the second forerunner of the coming of Christ, glorious Elijah sent grace from on high to Elisha, to dispel diseases and to cleanse lepers. Therefore, he pours forth healings on those who honor him.

signs and works had the same effect on many of His witnesses.

At one time, when Elijah feared for his life, he retreated into the desert for forty days and was sustained by God on very little food. Jesus underwent the same period of seclusion and fasting shortly before his death and Resurrection.

Elijah, though, was not actually to die. He was shown signs by God that renewed his faith, and some time later, after Ahab had been killed, a new king installed, and Elisha named as Elijah's successor, he was taken up to Heaven by a whirlwind in a chariot of fire. While this does not equate to Jesus' ultimate Ascension to Heaven—Elijah did not ascend by his own power—the similarity is a sign in itself.

There are three icons of Elijah at St. Nicholas. The icon in the dome is focused on Elijah's life. Elijah is dressed as an ascetic, a sojourner in the wilderness. His sandals, brown tunic, and green hair-lined cloak represent the simplicity and spirituality found in the retreats of the earth.

Elijah, who paralleled Jesus in his life and many of his deeds, has his right hand raised in the same Byzantine blessing that Jesus gives in the Pantocrator icon. His scroll reads, "As the Lord God of Moses the God of Israel lives," a passage that notes the continuity of the God Moses knew, He who Elijah knew, and the One we know.

Elisha and Elijah both appear on the iconostas, in the icon that depicts Elijah's being taken up to Heaven. Traditionally, this icon does not show Elijah's ascension exactly as it is described in Scripture, but the key details are all included.

Both Elijah, as a grey-bearded man, and Elisha, who is much younger, are present. Elisha's arms are open and his face is raised. His pose expresses prayer and worship in response to the miracle he is witnessing, but also sadness that his friend and mentor is leaving him. Elijah stretches one arm down to his successor, and holds his other hand open, as if to underline and accept his destination.

In the Bible, a "chariot of fire" appeared on the scene and Elijah actually ascended in a "whirlwind." Here Elijah is seated in the chariot itself (4 Kgd. 2:11). The image of Elijah seated in the chariot, rather than taken up in the whirlwind, is traditional.

The desert, where Elijah rose and where both prophets spent much of their lives and performed many of their wonders, is faithfully depicted in the icon. The stream of water at Elisha's feet suggests a passage of scripture in which, while on their way to the place of Elijah's departure, Elijah caused the river Jordan to part, allowing "the two of them [to cross] on dry ground" (4 Kgd. 2:7). This last sign from Elijah before his ascension reflects Moses' similar parting of the Red Sea. The continuity from one prophet to another, leading all the way to Jesus Christ, is expressed in details like the stream of water in this icon.

PROPHET ELIAS

Prophet Elisha

c. 875 BC

ELISHA SUCCEEDED ELIJAH, AND THROUGHOUT HIS life performed similar wonders and miracles. After he watched Elijah's being accepted into Heaven, Elisha went on to provide wholesome land, food, and water for cities stricken with famine and drought, give God's aid to Israel in times of war, and relieve the poverty of people in need. He also restored a widow's son to life and cured a man of leprosy (4 Kgd. 2-8). Many of these miracles opened peoples' eyes to the true God, and gave them strong faith in Him.

Elisha's last words foretold of Israel's victory against Syria, and his body, in its tomb, raised another dead man to life. Altogether, just like Elijah's, Elisha's life acted in itself as a prophecy of Jesus' time on earth.

The icon of Elisha in the dome shows him clothed in a purple-blue robe. This suggests that he has been graced with God's power and majesty, and is sanctioned to perform God's miraculous work. Elisha holds his fingers in the same blessing that Elijah gives, which in turn Jesus gives in the Pantocrator icon. He is visually connected to the prophet whose work he took up and the Savior that this work foretold.

Written on Elisha's scroll are his words of faithfulness to Elijah as the older prophet prepared to enter Heaven: "As the Lord lives and my soul lives I shall not leave thee" (4 Kgd. 2:4). Elisha's remaining by Elijah as he left the earth expresses the devotion asked of the followers of Christ.

FEAST DAY
June 14

KONTAKION
Tone 2. A prophet of God didst thou become when worthily thou hadst been vouch-safed a double portion of God's grace as Elijah's true companion, O Elisha, divinely-blest; and with him, thou unceasingly entreatest Christ God in behalf of us all.

Prophet Isaiah

c. 740 BC

WHILE ELIJAH AND ELISHA ARE BOTH NOTABLE for their prophetic deeds, Isaiah, who appears in the Bible shortly after Elisha's death, is a more traditional prophet of words. Isaiah advised Hezekiah, a God-fearing king, passing on God's answers to Hezekiah's prayers, fears, and doubts (4 Kgd. 19:1-19).

But Isaiah was also responsible for a long, written prophecy, found in the Book of Isaiah, which detailed Christ's coming to earth, and the salvation He will bring. Isaiah's name, in fact, refers to God's salvation. The prophecy comes from the "vision of Isaiah, … which he saw against Jerusalem and Judah in the Kingdom of Uzziah, Jotham, Ahaz, and Hezekiah, Kings of Judah"—it is the product of a long life, spanning four kingships (Is. 1:1).

Isaiah describes the errors and redemptions of Israel in the eras he witnessed, and then, looking forward, details the sinfulness of the human race and the arrival of the ultimate Redeemer. Isaiah's vision is a clear and detailed view into the events of the New Testament. His messianic prophecies are of singular importance. Isaiah prophesied the virgin birth and the suffering Messiah.

In his icon, Isaiah wears the same shades of blue and red as Jesus does in many of His iconic portrayals. Isaiah's eyes and right hand—note the position of his fingers—are raised to the Pantocrator. His appearance and pose indicate Jesus' presence and significance.

"Give ear, O Earth," Isaiah's scroll reminds us, "for the Lord hath spoken" (Is. 1:2).

FEAST DAY
May 9

KONTAKION
Tone 4. Having received the gift of prophecy, O Prophet-martyr Isaiah, herald of God, thou didst make clear to all under the sun the Incarnation of God by crying with a great voice: Behold the Virgin shall conceive in her womb.

Prophet Jonah *c. 775 BC*

JONAH, WHO TRADITION SAYS NARRATED HIS OWN experiences in the Book bearing his name, prefigures both Christ himself and humanity's need for Him. After three days in the belly of the whale Jonah was released; here his life foreshadows Christ's three days in the tomb and thus he is himself an important *type* or sign of Our Lord and His Resurrection. God called Jonah to preach repentance to the people of Nineveh. Jonah obeyed God's call, and arriving at that sinful city, he preached such a warning of destruction that the Ninevites "turned from their evil ways" and came back under God's goodwill (Jon. 3:10). His role as a leader and prophet who turned a race of people toward salvation makes Jonah a forerunner of Christ.

But Jonah's initial fear of God's calling, and his attempt to escape it, is a sign of very human weakness. Only through repentance and self-sacrifice was Jonah able to reunite with God and pursue his course to Nineveh. Even after his task was completed, Jonah continued to fear for his own fate, but was comforted by God's personal reassurance. Jonah's weakness and its strengthening in God reflects our own need for such strength, and foretells of the link between God and man fulfilled in the New Testament.

Jonah's humility is represented by his brown robe and bare feet. He holds his scroll like an offering to the Pantocrator: his appearance speaks his message of repentance. The prayer on the scroll, "I cried by reason of my affliction unto the Lord," is a further reminder of our need to lay out our sins and pains to God (Jon. 2:3).

FEAST DAY
September 21 (Greek) or 22 (Slavic)

TROPARION
Tone 3. To the Ninevites, thou wast a trumpet, blaring fearful threats of Heaven's judgments, at the which they repented with all their hearts; and from the sea-monster's belly didst thou foreshow the Lord's divine Resurrection to all the world. Hence, entreat Him to bring out of corruption all of us, who honour thee, O Jonah, as a friend of God.

Prophet Jeremiah *c. 625 BC*

Although Jeremiah is said to be the main author of the Third and Fourth Books of Kingdoms, his main prophecy is set forth in the Book of Jeremiah and foretells the conquering of Jerusalem by Babylon. After the Israelites were exiled in Babylon, Jeremiah penned his Lamentations for the fate of his people, and an *epistle*, or instructional letter, to help direct their behavior. Jeremiah is one of the main prophets who foretells of a "new covenant" which would bring forgiveness of sins.

Like Moses, Jeremiah was at first unsure of God's call for him to lead and prophesy, but with God's reassurance he followed the call (Je. 1:4-10).

Jeremiah's prophecy speaks of God's justice and mercy. While the suffering of the Israelites is acknowledged and lamented, the salvation of Gentiles and Jews alike is also promised to those who remain faithful and obedient to God through such trying times. Jeremiah also underwent persecution from some of those who heard his message, just as Jesus would centuries later.

In the icon, Jeremiah's robe is the same shade as Zephaniah's, and represents the period of war central to his life and prophecy. The blessing he makes with his right hand indicates the One whose promise of peace and salvation we are to have faith in.

The phrase on his scroll, "Then the word of the Lord came," is repeated throughout the Book of Jeremiah, and emphasizes Jeremiah's connection to God and the truth of his prophecy.

FEAST DAY
May 1

KONTAKION
Tone 8. O blessed Jeremiah, being chosen of God from thy mother's womb, in thy compassion, thou sorely didst mourn for the falling away of Israel. And in Egypt, O Prophet, thou wast murdered by stoning for thy most just rebukes by them that understood not to cry with thee: Alleluia.

Prophet Habbakuk *c. 610 BC*

ABBAKUK, WHO LIVED AND PROPHESIED AT the same time as Zephaniah, Jeremiah, and Daniel, was painfully aware of the sin and suffering those other prophets also witnessed. In the Book of Habbakuk, the prophet cries out against the injustices of his human rulers and pleads for God to show justice.

In turn, God answers that the unjust men will be toppled and humbled by other men, and that in this way His work will be done and the sinners brought to repentance. When Habbakuk further questions God, He reveals how in due course the righteous will be protected and justified and the evildoers dealt with justly.

Habbakuk makes a brief Scriptural appearance in the story of Daniel, when he is carried by an angel to minister to the prophet Daniel in the lions' den (Da. 22:33).

The hand of Habbakuk in the icon, raised as if to cover his face, suggests his initial dismay. The drab, muted green he wears also conveys a sense of sadness. But Habbakuk is also clothed in red and blue; God is present with him. His scroll, too, recognizes God's presence even in a time of uncertainty. When Habbakuk prayed, "O Lord, I have heard thy speech and was afraid," he was expressing his inability to fully understand God's plan, but assuring that he believed in it (Hb. 3:2).

FEAST DAY
December 2

KONTAKION

Tone 4. Thou plainly beheldest the sacred disciples of Christ as horses that troubled the deep sea of ignorance, plunging error into the depths with their godly teachings, Habbakuk, God-proclaimer; hence, as a true Prophet, we acclaim thee, while asking that thou shouldst intercede that we find mercy with God the Lord.

Prophet Daniel

c. 600 BC

DANIEL LIVED WITH HIS PEOPLE'S LEADERS IN captivity in Babylon. He began spreading the word of God to both the Jews and their captors when he was very young. He first spoke God's truth when he revealed the innocence of Susanna, an Israelite princess unjustly accused of immoral conduct (Sus. 1-63), and from that point on maintained a strong presence amid Babylonian royalty. His signs and his interpretation of their visions led kings of Babylon to recognize, understand, and follow the true God. Daniel, along with several of his peers, was protected by God from multiple attempts on his life.

The Book of Daniel, as well as describing these events, contains Daniel's huge and detailed prophecy. Daniel covers the human events of kings and wars that will unfold throughout the centuries, and the progress of Israel leading up to the birth of Jesus. Daniel's prophecy also elaborately symbolizes both the two comings of Christ. His prophecy that "the Son of Man was coming with the clouds of heaven" is an important prophecy of the Second Coming. (Da. 7:13)

As Daniel spoke and acted on God's behalf so significantly in his youth, he is portrayed in the icon as a young man. Like his three young friends and fellow prophets, who were saved by God from fire, Daniel is dressed in a cap and leg coverings (Da. 3:21). His scroll, reading "The God of Heaven shall set up a kingdom," comes from near the beginning of Daniel's prophecy. The full passage describes how God's kingdom will outlast the unstable kingdoms of earth (Da. 2:44).

FEAST DAY
December 17

KONTAKION

Tone 3. Since thy pure and hallowed heart had been made pure by the Spirit, it became His dwelling-place and clearest prophecy's vessel; for thou didst behold things far off as near and present, and when cast into the den, thou didst muzzle lions; for which cause, O blessed Prophet, glorious Daniel, we all revere thee in faith.

Prophet Ezekiel

c. 600 BC

FEAST DAY
July 21 (Slavic), July 23 (Greek)

KONTAKION
Tone 4. O divine Ezekiel, as God's true Prophet, thou foretoldest unto all the Incarnation of the Lord, the Lamb of God, the Artificer, the Son of God, the Eternal made manifest.

THE PROPHET EZEKIEL WAS A LEVITE WHO GREW up during King Josiah's reign and prophesied in the same era as Daniel and Jeremiah. He is the author of the Book of Ezekiel, which records the setting and content of his prophecies in great detail.

Ezekiel was sent elaborate visions by God. The images he saw represented the coming of Jesus, the Virgin Mary, and the great importance of righteous saints and writers of Scripture. In fact, Ezekiel's very first vision seems an image of the ideal Church, with Jesus as the center of knowledge and virtue (Ez. 1). God also called Ezekiel to place himself in confinement for a time, taking on the sins of Israel, so that he made himself into an image of Jesus (Ez. 2).

But Ezekiel was also given more specific prophecies, which he was to pass on to the Israelites even though, as God said, they were "unwilling to listen to Me" (Ez. 3:7). Ezekiel told of Israel's sins, its upcoming captivity, and the destruction in surrounding regions. But all through Ezekiel's visions and prophecies were reminders that God would not abandon His people however much they strayed. Also, Ezekiel himself was made able to call sinners to repentance.

By speaking God's truth in the face of opposition, Ezekiel was a forerunner of Jesus Christ.

Ezekiel is shown humbly dressed, bending in deference to the Pantocrator as he raises his hand in blessing. The passage on his scroll, "Thus saith the Lord behold I will search out my sheep," comes from a prophecy that illustrates God's devotion to His scattered, straying, and wounded people.

Prophet Zechariah   *c. 525 BC*

ZECHARIAH WAS BORN INTO CAPTIVITY IN BABY-
lon, but went back to Judah before his life was
over. His prophecy focuses on the rebuilding of the Temple in Israel, which the Babylonians had destroyed, and
the events of the next five centuries leading up to Jesus'
birth.

Zechariah's prophecy is the last by the Prophets
portrayed on the dome, and in a way fulfills the prophecies that have come before it. His vision prefigures the
events of Jesus's life in great detail, giving a shape to God's
earlier promises of salvation which preceded it.

In the icon Zechariah is clothed in the familiar blue
and red that call to mind the garments of Jesus in the icons
depicting Him. He is shown with his pen still positioned
on the blank half of his scroll. His words "Thus saith the
Lord," though they open the prophecy in the Book of
Zechariah, also declare the prophecy's meaning final.

But Zechariah has either just finished writing these
words, or he is still in the process of writing them. The
fulfillment of his prophecy is so near, that there is not
time for his ink to dry. The space on his scroll for more
writing signals the fulfillment to come soon.

This fulfillment begins with the birth of Jesus
Christ.

FEAST DAY
February 8

KONTAKION

Tone 4. As a brightly-shining lamp that
was illumined with the Spirit's fiery
beams, O Zechariah most renowned,
thou didst prefigure with clarity the
Savior's great and untold condescen-
sion toward us.

64 Deacon Clement Nicoloff reads the Gospel, one of the foremost icons of Jesus Christ

64-65 The Divine Liturgy's Great Entrance, which symbolizes Christ's entry into Jerusalem

Culmination of the Ages

THE NEW TESTAMENT

The Virgin Mary *c. 20 BC – 1ˢᵗ century AD*

ERHAPS THE MOST EYE-CATCHING ICON IN THE SANCTU-
ary is found on the upper half of the *apse*, the domed space
behind the altar. It shows the Virgin Mary, who is known in the
Orthodox Church as the *Theotokos* (Greek for "Birthgiver of God"
or "Mother of God"), seated with the child Jesus. Both Mother
and Son have their arms outstretched. This icon shows Mary as
the *Platytera*, meaning "more spacious."

The "spaciousness" expressed in this icon is the "spaciousness" of Mary's womb. Although Mary is fully human, and gave
birth to Jesus Christ as a human mother giving birth to a human
son, through the grace of God she bore the Son of God in His
divinity. Her womb "more spacious than the Heavens," Mary miraculously bears the God who holds the universe in the palm of
His hand.

Every aspect of this particular icon, from its size and setting
to the stars on Mary's mantle and the position of Jesus' fingers,
illuminates Mary's role in God's becoming man, and the divine
significance of this act. The dome of the apse represents, like the
center dome, the fullness of Heaven. The gold leaf background
suggests holiness and glory. Mary is dressed as she always is in
Orthodox iconography: her head is covered in the fashion of a
young maiden; her blue robe, which represents purity and virtue, is worn under a red mantle, which represents the divine God
whom she bore. In some icons, three gold stars are painted on
the front of Mary's veil, but here they adorn her shoulders and
forehead. The three stars demonstrate, wherever they are placed,
Mary's ever-virginity before, during, and after the birth of Christ.
The ever-virginity of the Theotokos is another sign that God, in

becoming Man, overcame the limitations of nature, and it also reflects the enduring purity of the Church as the vessel of the Holy Spirit.

Mary's outstretched arms, in the form of an embrace, not only gesture the spaciousness of her womb, but also place her in a position of prayer. The circle, or *nimbus*, around her head is a sign of holiness, and the Greek monograms on either side of her, *MP ΘY*, represent the Greek title *Mētēr tou Theou*, or *Mother of God*.

She presents her Son to the world as Lord.

Jesus' arms are also outstretched to us as well, and His fingers are raised in the same Byzantine blessing that represents God's nature. He is labeled with the Greek monogram *IC XC*, for *Jesus Christ*. The cross in His nimbus identifies Him as well.

The faces of both Mary and Jesus express power and serenity. In iconography, the young Jesus is depicted as a miniature adult rather than a child, indicating His changelessness. The unusual breadth and height of his forehead show His great wisdom.

Icons like this *Platytera* also belong to a wider category, called *Orans* or *The Virgin of the Sign*, in reference to fulfillment of the "sign" prophesied by Isaiah that a virgin shall conceive and bear a son. In any *Orans* icon, Mary appears as a worshipper of God. Here, she glorifies God and, with her Son, shows us the nature of that glory.

On the iconostasis, Mary is more specifically shown as the Mother of God *(opposite)*. While the larger icon demonstrates the vastness and power of God, this one shows us the way to God and Salvation.

This icon is an example of Mary as *Hodigitria*, or *She Who Shows the Way*. Like all icons of its type, it is based on what is traditionally held to be the first icon of Mary ever painted, by St. Luke. With her attire, monogram, and face, she is immediately recognizable as the Virgin Mary and *Theotokos*. She holds the child Jesus, but while other icons may show her embracing and comforting him as a mother would, here He sits upright. Jesus, dressed in gold and giving a blessing with His right hand, is enthroned in Mary's arms. With her own right hand, Mary points to Jesus, displaying him as the Son of the One True God and our path to Salvation.

Because of the *Hodigitria* icon's traditional place on the iconostasis to the left of the Holy Doors, Mary also appears to be gesturing with her hand and posture to the icon of Our Lord on the right side of the Holy Doors.

The Holy Doors themselves further link these icons of the Theotokos and Jesus Christ, with their portrayal of the Annunciation from God (p. 70), that the Virgin Mary would give birth to His Son.

September 8, November 21, March 25, and August 15

The Annunciation to Mary   *c. 5 BC*

As St. Luke describes in his Gospel, the Annunciation took place as "the angel Gabriel was sent by God to a city of Galilee named Nazareth," and there spoke to the Virgin Mary (Lk. 1:26-27). Gabriel reassured the bemused Mary that she had "found favor with God," and would "conceive in your womb and bring forth a Son," who would be called Jesus (Lk. 1:30-31) The ultimate response of the Theotokos to God's messenger, "Let it be to me according to your word" (Lk. 1:38) marks the conception of He who is fully God and fully man. As the Troparion of the Feast of the Annunciation (March 25) proclaims, "Today is the beginning of our salvation, the revelation of the eternal mystery! The Son of God becomes the Son of the Virgin as Gabriel announces the coming of Grace. Together with him let us cry to the Theotokos: Rejoice, O Full of Grace, the Lord is with you!"

The Annunciation appears twice in the icons of St. Nicholas. First, an icon of the Annunciation adorns the front of the Holy Doors in the center of the iconostas (*next page*). These doors separate the sanctuary from the rest of the church. The placement of the icon of the Annunciation here reminds us that the Theotokos opens the door of salvation through her

consent to bear the Son of God, so that "all generations" will call her "blessed." In this way the Holy Doors themselves "announce" the presence of Christ among us during the Divine Liturgy. Both the Gospel and Holy Communion, the word of God and the body and blood of Christ, are brought to us through them.

In this icon, we recognize the Archangel Gabriel and the Virgin Mary from other icons in the church, but here they appear together, Gabriel raising his hand in greeting, blessing and announcement, and Mary opening her hands to receive the news and accept the role God has chosen for her, establishing a New Covenant in this very act of obedience. The Holy Spirit is depicted as a bright blue stream descending toward Mary, anointing her. The icon of the Annunciation on the Holy Doors proclaims the Incarnation through reminding us that the Theotokos opens the gates for the coming of Grace, just as the Holy Doors open for the coming of the very body and blood of Christ Himself.

The second icon of the Annunciation, located on the north wall to the left of the iconostasis (*opposite*), shows the same event in greater detail. It also marks the first in a series of large "festal" icons which ring the walls of the church

from left to right and mark several Great Feasts of the Orthodox Church, commemorating events in the life and Jesus and the Church from the Annunciation through Pentecost.

Here, in the larger of the two Annunciation icons, the city walls in the background suggest not only the city of Nazareth but also the world itself, now touched and changed forever by the Incarnation announced by the Angel. Mary is seated in what resembles, in style and colors of red, blue and gold, both an altar and a throne. In one hand, she holds a spool of thread. Tradition tells us that when the An-

nunciation took place, Mary was weaving or mending the veil of the Holy of Holies in the Temple.

Mary is elevated slightly above Gabriel, who is bent at the knee in praise of the one he "hails" who has "found favor with God." His outstretched arm and the blue ray of the Holy Spirit descending on her direct our attention to the one who is "full of grace." Mary is clearly the central figure of the icon; yet, her pose is one of humility and acceptance. She neither boasts in her exaltation, nor shudders at the prospect of doing God's will.

Father Daniel Daly, holding
a palm frond, teaches the
children on Palm Sunday

The Nativity of Christ

WHEN MARY'S TIME CAME TO GIVE birth, she and her husband Joseph traveled from Nazareth to the city of Bethlehem. There, because the local inn was full, they were given a place to stay among the inn's animals. In Orthodox tradition, Jesus Christ was born in a cave.

As Jesus was born, God sent signs to the world of His Son's arrival. To the humble shepherds who were doing their work nearby, God sent angels to give the good news. To the learned wise men who were sent by their king to assess the situation, God gave a star that guided them on their journey. Both groups learned of the Nativity of Jesus, and were brought to new understanding and faith in the true God. The troparion hymn for the feast of Nativity, or Christmas (December 25), describes how "Thy Nativity, O Christ our God, hath given rise to the light of knowledge in the world."

Our Nativity icon follows the tradition of showing the Baby Jesus laid inside a cave. On either side of him are an ox and an ass, animals that appear in Isaiah's prophecy (Is. 1:3).

Mary sits just in front of Him, expressing adoration and tenderness. Both Mary and Jesus are identified by their Greek monograms.

Below Mary sits her betrothed, the righteous Joseph. While some icons will clearly show the doubts Joseph underwent as his wife gave birth, in this one he is tired and care-worn, but clearly accepting of the event at hand.

The angels surrounding the cave appear to be attending the birth, serving the Son of God. Another angel gives the good news to the shepherds, who respond with wonder. Even their sheep are in awe, as is nature itself. The wise men are shown in the background, traveling toward the city of Bethlehem, clearly led by the symbol of the Holy Spirit that doubles as a star. The Holy Spirit also descends upon Jesus.

The format of the Nativity icon, with Jesus placed centrally and all other figures arranged to draw attention to Him, is repeated in most other festal icons. The next icon chronologically, and the next icon on the wall, is the icon of Theophany, or the Baptism of Jesus.

The Theophany of Christ

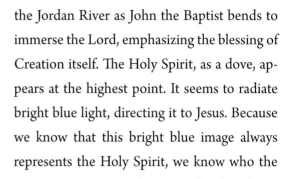

ON THE FEAST OF THEOPHANY (January 6), we celebrate the Baptism of Jesus. Not only did Jesus' baptism set the precedent for how all of us who follow Him will be baptized, it was also the first time that all three persons of the Holy Trinity were clearly revealed to those present at the same time. "Theophany" is Greek for "appearance of God."

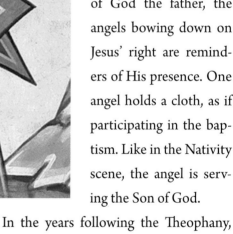

When Jesus had grown to adulthood, He was baptized in the river Jordan by his cousin John, who we know as John the Baptist (p. 78). As Jesus the Son stood in the river, the "heavens were opened," the Holy Spirit came down in the form of a dove, and God the Father was heard saying, "This is my beloved Son, in whom I am well pleased" (Mt. 3:16). At this time, as the second phrase of the troparion hymn of Theophany tells, "the worship of the Trinity was made manifest," as all three members appeared together.

The icon portrays the events of Theophany as fully as a silent image can. Jesus stands in the Jordan River as John the Baptist bends to immerse the Lord, emphasizing the blessing of Creation itself. The Holy Spirit, as a dove, appears at the highest point. It seems to radiate bright blue light, directing it to Jesus. Because we know that this bright blue image always represents the Holy Spirit, we know who the dove is in the Theophany icon.

While it is impossible to show the voice of God the father, the angels bowing down on Jesus' right are reminders of His presence. One angel holds a cloth, as if participating in the baptism. Like in the Nativity scene, the angel is serving the Son of God.

In the years following the Theophany, Jesus gathered His Apostles and disciples, and traveled throughout the area teaching God's wisdom and performing signs and miracles. The icons of the Apostles are located on the top row of the iconostas.

John the Baptist is also depicted on the iconostas.

Saint John the Baptist

JOHN THE BAPTIST, SOMETIMES KNOWN as the Forerunner of Christ, is the great prophet of the New Testament, and fulfilled many prophecies of those who came before him. He was the son of the Virgin Mary's barren cousin Elizabeth and her husband Zacharias. The conception and birth of John reflected that of many Old Testament prophets, and also signed the birth of Our Lord.

When he grew up, John the Baptist retreated into the desert and lived as an ascetic prophet. He "was clothed in camel's hair, with a leather belt around his waist" (Mt. 3:4). As Isaiah prophesied, John came on his countrymen as the "the voice of one crying in the wilderness "to make themselves ready for Jesus' coming" (Mt. 3:2). Many answered John's call to repentance and were baptized by him.

Finally, Jesus Himself came to be baptized by John. John was reluctant at first, thinking himself unworthy, but performed the sacra-

ment with Jesus' permission. The Holy Trinity was made manifest in the great Theophany, which John witnessed.

For the rest of his life, St. John remained a prophet and a teacher. He was martyred by Herod the Tetrarch, beheaded at the request of Herod's wife.

On the iconostas, John wears the ascetic robe described in Scripture. His feet are bare, and his hair and beard are unruly. He is clearly a sojourner in the wilderness.

Our icon of St. John illuminates his prophecy. The phrase on his scroll, "Repent for the kingdom of God is at hand," is from his own call to the people before the Son of God began His ministry. With his right hand he makes the blessing of Christ and the Trinity, and as Christ's Forerunner also points to the icon of Our Lord in His second coming. In this way we are reminded that Jesus is as much the Way to Salvation now as He was during the time of St. John the Baptist.

SAINT JOHN   THE BAPTIST

REPENT
FOR THE
KINGDM
OF GOD
IS AT
HAND

The Apostles

THEIR VOICE HATH GONE OUT INTO ALL THE EARTH

ACROSS THE TOP ROW OF THE ICONOSTAS ARE the icons of the *Apostles*, Jesus' core group of followers, and the *Evangelists*, the writers of the Gospels. All of the Apostles were faithful to Jesus during His life and had active roles in founding the Church after Pentecost. Except for St. John, all of the Apostles were martyred, professing their faith unto death. Along with their individual feast days, the Apostles are all commemorated together on January 30.

Icons of the four Evangelists, Sts. Matthew, Mark, Luke and John (Matthew and John were Apostles as well), are also found on the *pendentives*, the four corners below the dome. As the Prophets above them spoke of Jesus' coming to the world, the Evangelists wrote of His words and deeds after He came into the world.

80-81   The reading of the *Epistles*, the letters written by the Apostles, is an important time of instruction in the Divine Liturgy.

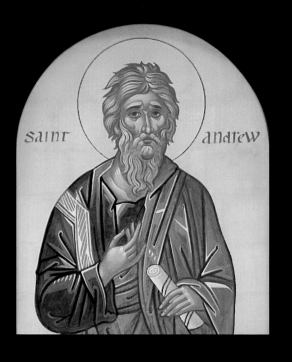

saint andrew

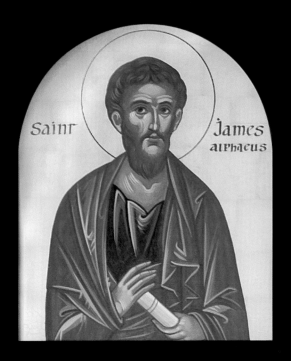

saint james alphaeus

Saint Mark the Evangelist

WHILE NOT HIMSELF ONE OF THE Twelve Apostles, the Evangelist St. Mark is said to have been present at Jesus' arrest. In the Gospel of Mark, the "young man" who ran away from the scene, and apparently watched the Crucifixion from afar, may have been Mark himself (Mk. 14:51). Mark's is the only Gospel to mention this young man, and he may very well have been describing his own involvement.

Mark became more active in the ministry following the Ascension, and was a disciple of both Paul and Peter. Because Peter was one of the Twelve, Mark was probably influenced by his testimony as he wrote his Gospel around AD 70.

Mark was appointed by St. Peter as the first bishop in Egypt, and spread the Gospel there, establishing the Church of Alexandria.

He was driven away by the pagans twice, and returned. Two years later he was martyred.

Although St. Mark did know Jesus, his Gospel tends to be told instead from Peter's point of view. It also highlights Jesus' role as "the Son of Man" who "did not come to be served, but to serve" (Mk. 10:45).

The large icons of the four Evangelists are located on the *pendentives* in each corner, in the space just below the dome. This arrangement represents the "four corners of the Earth," the whole world to which the Evangelists brought the Good News. Mark is on the left, on the side closest to the iconostas.

The depiction of St. Mark writing his Gospel in the dome is identical to the one on the iconostas. Even the colors of his robes are the same. In both icons, he is clearly himself, and clearly an Evangelist.

SAINT mark

FEAST DAY
April 25

KONTAKION

Tone 2. When thou hadst received the Spirit's grace from Heaven's heights, thou rentest apart the webs of the philosophers; and on catching all of the nations in thy net, O all-lauded Mark, thou didst offer them to thy Lord, by preaching the Gospel of divine renown.

Saint Matthew the Evangelist

MATTHEW THE EVANGELIST, ALSO CALLED Levi, also appears both among the icons of the Apostles and on the *pendentives* beneath the dome. As one of the Twelve Apostles, he witnessed the works and miracles of Jesus, and is traditionally held to have described those in the Gospel of his name.

When he was called to be an Apostle, Matthew was working as a tax collector. Jesus' choice to befriend a tax collector, which was seen as a sinful profession, surprised many people, but it taught Jesus' lesson of forgiveness and acceptance.

After Pentecost, St. Matthew spent his ministry in various places, and is thought to have written his Gospel in Antioch between AD 50 and 70. He was martyred in Ethiopia.

The Gospel of St. Matthew shows a deep understanding of Jewish law and tradition. Matthew's focus was on how Jesus, with His coming, fulfilled and reinterpreted these traditions in a new way.

The two icons of St. Matthew clearly show the same man, though in the icon on the *pendentive* he is slightly older. On the iconostas, he holds an open Gospel. The gold, jeweled book resembles the same ornate Gospel books used in many Orthodox churches.

Below the dome, St. Matthew is shown in the process of writing his Gospel. His paper and writing tools are laid out on the table beside him. Like the other Evangelists, he writes in Greek, the original language of the New Testament.

FEAST DAY
November 16

KONTAKION

Tone 4. When thou didst cast away the publican's balance and wast united to the yoke of uprightness, then didst thou prove a merchant of great excellence, one that gathered in the wealth of the wisdom of Heaven; for this cause, the word of truth thou didst herald, O Matthew, and didst arouse the souls of sluggish men by signifying the dread day of reckoning.

Saint Peter

PETER, A CHIEF APOSTLE ALONG WITH St. Paul, was originally called Simon. The name *Peter* and his title *Cephas* both mean *rock*, and were both given by Jesus. Peter's declaration of faith was the "Rock," the foundation, on which the Church would be built. He was first called alongside his brother Andrew.

Peter's betrayal of Jesus when He was arrested and about to be crucified is memorable. Peter was so afraid for his own safety that he three times denied that he even knew Jesus. But Peter sincerely repented of his action, and was forgiven.

After Pentecost, he became a vocal and courageous leader of the new faith. He traveled throughout the Mediterranean, which for a man of his time and place made up much of the known world. His acts are a large part of the Acts of the Apostles.

St. Peter was condemned to death by Nero, and installed St. Linus as bishop of Rome. He went cheerfully to his death, crucified upside-down, having truly lived up to his name as a solid foundation of the Church.

St. Peter, in gold, holds in his icon a scroll that is unfurling. The Word of God is become manifest in the Church St. Peter helped found. With his right hand, he doubly shows the scroll's importance. Not only does he point to the scroll, but he points with his two raised fingers. The scroll is the Way, and the Way is the Human and Divine Son of God, Jesus Christ.

Across from St. Peter, on the other side of the Holy Doors, is the icon of St. Paul, another great founder of a number of churches. Sts. Peter and Paul share a feast day, June 29, and a troparion hymn that calls them "O foremost in the ranks of the Apostles and teachers of the world."

KONTAKION

Tone 2. Today Christ the Rock glorifies with highest honor the rock of Faith and leader of the Apostles, together with Paul and the company of the twelve, whose memory we celebrate with eagerness of faith, giving glory to the one who gave glory to them!

Saint Paul

ALTHOUGH ST. PAUL WAS NOT ONE OF THE original Apostles, he is known today as a chief Apostle, and his works were vital in the Church's beginning.

Paul, known at that time as Saul, was actively engaged in the persecution of the early Church. But, while traveling to Damascus in search of believers to arrest, he was struck with a vision of Christ and made blind for several days. Shaken, Saul repented of his actions, and was moved to convert to the same faith he had persecuted. As he was baptized, his sight was restored. Eventually he was given the name Paul, and became a strong Christian leader and teacher.

Like all the Apostles, Paul suffered persecution himself, and was placed under house arrest in Rome. During this long period, Paul performed his ministry from a distance. He continued to write letters to a large network of developing churches and disciples. While Paul dealt with problems and issues specific to the people and communities he wrote to at the time, many of these topics are still relevant to the faithful today. Paul's *epistles*, or letters, are now a significant part of the New Testament. Having left this written legacy behind him, St. Paul was finally martyred in Rome.

St. Paul's high, round forehead and pointed beard are easily recognized in any of his icons. Like the Evangelists, he holds a Gospel, as if offering it outward. He and St. Peter, facing each other, are oriented toward the Holy Doors and altar. As the two chief Apostles, Sts. Peter and Paul are often shown together in iconography. In this arrangement, even though they are not in the same icon, they still appear to be united.

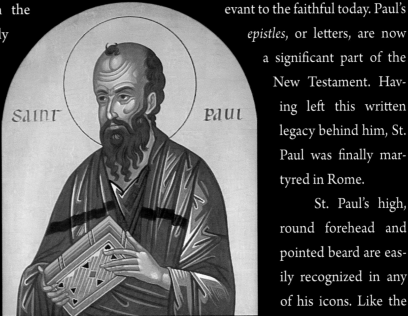

KONTAKION

Tone 2. O Lord, Thou hast taken up to eternal rest and to the enjoyment of Thy blessings the two divinely-inspired preachers, the leaders of the Apostles, for Thou hast accepted their labors and deaths as a sweet-smelling sacrifice, for Thou alone knowest what lies in the hearts of men.

SAINT JOHN

Saint John the Evangelist

JOHN THE EVANGELIST DID NOT ONLY author a Gospel, but was a much-beloved Apostle and minister of Jesus. He and his brother James were both fishermen and both called by Jesus at the same time and place. Jesus also gave him the surname *Boanerges*, "Son of Thunder."

John witnessed the Transfiguration and remained at Jesus' side when He was crucified. At His crucifixion, Our Lord entrusted John with the care of His mother Mary.

After Pentecost, St. John became a Church leader in Ephesus. He wrote his Gospel while there near the end of his life. John is also said to to have authored the Book of Revelation not long after, when he was exiled on the Greek island of Patmos. The only Apostle who was not martyred, St. John died a natural death in AD 100.

The Gospel of St. John, the latest of the four Gospels, emphasizes that Jesus is the true Son of God and the path to salvation. Our salvation through the Resurrection is especially emphasized. For these reasons the Orthodox Church also knows St. John as "the Theologian."

St. John appears on the iconostas among the Apostles and on the pendentives among the Evangelists. He is also found in in the icons of the Transfiguration and Crucifixion. The festal icons show him as a very young man, but those that portry him as an individual show him later in life. On the iconostas, he holds the Gospel, which identifies him as an Evangelist. On the *pendentive*, on the right and nearest the iconostas, St. John is shown writing the Gospel.

saint · john

FEAST DAY
May 8

TROPARION

Tone 2. Beloved Apostle of Christ our God, hasten to deliver a people without defense. He who permitted you to recline upon His bosom, accepts you on bended knee before Him. Beseech Him, O Theologian, to dispel the persistent cloud of nations, asking for us peace and great mercy.

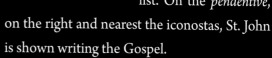

Saint Luke the Evangelist

Like St. Mark, St. Luke was not one of the Twelve Apostles, but was one of the the four Evangelists. He was a Gentile, not a Jew, born in Antioch. He was a physician by profession.

Luke became a disciple of St. Paul and traveled with Paul and Peter throughout the Mediterranean. Under Paul's supervision, he wrote his Gospel in the years 62 and 63. As Luke had participated in the building of the early Church, he described those events in the Acts of the Apostles, which he also authored.

Luke was a Gentile. His Gospel is written to show that salvation through Jesus Christ is universal and open to all people, not only the Jews. The Gospel of Luke is also concerned with histori-cal accuracy and carefully notes when events took place.

Besides writing his Gospel and the Book of Acts, Luke evangelized in another very important way. He is said to have painted images of Mary the Theotokos, and of Sts. Peter and Paul. He can be called the first iconographer, and our icons today are based on his first paintings.

St. Luke died a natural death at the age of 86 in Achaia in western Greece.

Like the two icons of St. Mark, the two icons of St. Luke clearly show the same man. He holds a Gospel book and makes a blessing. In the icon below the dome on the *pendentive*, on the right toward the entrance to the sanctuary, St. Luke is shown seated, in the process of writing.

saint luke

FEAST DAYS
October 18 and June 20

KONTAKION
Tone 5. Let us praise with sacred songs the Holy Apostle Luke, the recorder of the Joyous Gospel of Christ, and the scribe of the Acts of the Apostles, for his writings are a testimony of the Church of Christ: he is the Physician of human weaknesses and infirmities. He heals the wounds of our souls, and constantly intercedes for our salvation!

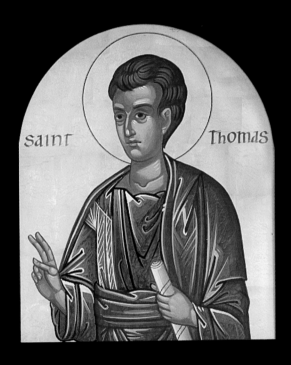

IC XC

The raising of Adam

The Ascension of Christ

URING THE FORTY DAYS AFTER HIS RESurrection, Jesus preached final words of joy and encouragement to his disciples, instructing them to bring news of salvation "To the end of the earth" (Acts 1:8). On the fortieth day, Jesus "was taken up, and a cloud received Him out of their sight," (Acts 1:9). The disciples then saw a vision of two angels, "men in white," who told them that "This same Jesus" would one day return to earth "in like manner as you saw him go into heaven" (Acts 1:11).

The feast of the Ascension, Christ's glorious return to heaven after restoring fallen humanity, is appropriately celebrated forty days after Pascha. The troparion hymn of the feast sings the praises and significance of the event: "Thou hast ascended with glory, O Christ our God, and hast gladdened the Disciples with the promise of the Holy Spirit; making them confident through the blessing that Thou art the Son of God, and Deliverer of the world."

The icon shows Jesus Christ "ascending with glory," dressed in gold and seated in the blue nimbus of the Holy Spirit, being raised up by angels. His fulfilling of the Word of God is represented by the scroll in His hand.

The disciples are gathered below Him, watching in amazement. The two angels in white direct their attention, and ours, up toward Jesus. The Theotokos stands in the center, calmly facing outward and raising her hands once more to present her Son.

Now that Jesus had departed the earth after His First Coming, His disciples would go forth to build the base of the Church, just as they build the visual base of the icon. Ten days after Jesus Ascended into heaven, they would receive the Holy Spirit so they could achieve this.

Pentecost

Before His Ascension Jesus made three promises to His disciples: that the Father would send the Comforter, the Holy Spirit to them; that It would lead them into all Truth; and that It would remain with them forever. All these things came to pass fifty days after the Resurrection, on the Day of Pentecost (Acts 2:1), and form the foundation of the Church and the basis of its continuing ministry today.

On this day, as a large group of disciples were gathered together, "there came a sound from heaven, as of a rushing mighty wind," and "there appeared to them divided tongues, as of fire, and one sat upon each of them" (Acts 2:2-3). These forces of purification were signs of God's presence among the disciples, and this blessing of them to do His work. As the disciples "were all filled with the Holy Spirit" "they began to speak with other tongues" "as the Spirit gave them utterance" (Acts 2:4). The gift of knowing other languages was not only an important practical ability for the disciples to have as they began their ministries, but also represented the unity of all people, regardless of language, in Christ.

As the Troparion for Pentecost, whose feast is celebrated fifty days after Pascha, proclaims, Christ "didst reveal the fisherman as most wise, having sent upon them the Holy Spirit, and through them thou has fished the universe," and drawn the universe nearer to God.

The icon shows the twelve Apostles seated together, with the tongues of flame upon their heads and the Holy Spirit present above them. Below them, emerging from a dark cave of uncertainty, is a generic king who personifies the world. The king reaches his cloth up to the light. It contains twelve rolled scrolls, which hold the salvation about to be revealed by the disciples as they "fish the universe."

The founding of the Church opened the way for the acts and sacrifices of many saints and martyrs who are depicted in the icons of St. Nicholas.

114 The Church remembers the death and burial of Christ in a solemn vigil service on Holy Friday.

114-115 The people recieve the Body and Blood of Christ.

The Church Era

THOU HAST FISHED
THE UNIVERSE

As the first bishop of Jerusalem, the Apostle James, "the brother of the Lord," has his place among the icons of the Church Fathers. These men, all early bishops and leaders, all played key roles in the Church's development and defense. The icons are painted behind the altar, as a reminder of the Fathers' development of Holy Tradition and the Liturgy.

James was not actually the Lord's brother, as Mary remained a virgin throughout her life. But he is thought to be either the son of Joseph from an earlier marriage, or another relation. James was one of Jesus' disciples, and went on to become Jerusalem's first bishop and lead the early council that took place there, at which it was confirmed that salvation was to extend beyond the Jews, to the Gentiles. He is also credited for writing the Divine Liturgy of St. James. He was condemned by the Jewish Sanhedrin and stoned in AD 62.

Like the other Church Fathers, St. James is dressed as a priest. The words on his scroll, "Lord, Lord, look down from Heaven on this your vineyard," come originally from a parable, comparing the Church and the world to God's vineyard, that St. James would have heard from Our Lord Himself. The line is from a liturgical prayer said by a bishop for the welfare of his diocese.

FEAST DAY
October 23

SAINT GEORGE

FEAST DAY
December 4

Saint Barbara the Great Martyr

c. 280 – 306

BARBARA, BORN IN THE THIRD CENTUry in Syria, was so beautiful that her pagan father placed her in an isolated tower to keep her innocent of any influence except his own until she could be married. Like St. Christina, Barbara also came to realize that the idols she saw were not real gods, and determined to live in celibacy and devotion for the Creator.

Barbara's father was troubled by her new beliefs, and hoped to distract her by sending her into civilization. But Barbara instead befriended several young Christian women who taught her their beliefs, and was baptized herself. After undergoing great torture and being healed with visions of Christ, St. Barbara, alongside the virgin St. Juliana, who was inspired by compassion to join her, was martyred by her own father in 306.

The icon of St. Barbara shows her crowned with her virginity and martyrdom, and ornately dressed. Like other martyrs, she holds a cross.

SAINT NICHOLAS

To this man the gate-keeper opens and he calls his own sheep by name and leads them forth

Saint Nicholas the Wonderworker

c. 270–343

Nicholas was born in the third century in the city of Patara. His wealthy Christian parents died when he was young, and he gave his inheritance to the poor. Devoting himself to the Church, Nicholas was eventually ordained Bishop of Myra.

In this position of responsibility, St. Nicholas proved himself to be extremely kind and generous. He is known today for using whatever resources he had to aid people in need, though during his life he was careful to keep his identity a secret. One of the most famous stories of his generosity tells of his tossing three bags of gold through the window of a poor man with three daughters. Nicholas gave enough to pay for the marriages of all three girls.

In his public life, Nicholas lived through the reign of the anti-Christian emperor Diocletian. Nicholas was imprisoned for his faith, but survived and was eventually released.

He attended the Council of Nicea in AD 325, also called the First Ecumenical Council, where the Nicene Creed was drafted. There he famously stood against the heretic Arius, who taught that Jesus was a created being.

St. Nicholas is called "Wonderworker" for his many miracles. By his prayers and actions, famines were lifted, prisoners were set free, and diseases were healed.

At an old age, St. Nicholas died a natural death. He is commemorated on December 6.

As the patron saint of our parish church, St. Nicholas is assigned a special place on the iconostas, to the right of the Virgin Mary as *Hodigitria*.

In this icon, St. Nicholas appears in his bishop's vestments. He gives a blessing with one hand, and with the other holds an open book that reads "To this man the gatekeeper opens and he calls his own sheep by name and leads them forth." This is a passage from the Book of John, where Jesus describes how He is the way to salvation.

FEAST DAY
December 6

TROPARION

Tone 4. The truth of things revealed thee to thy flock as a rule of faith, a model of meekness, and a teacher of temperance. Therefore thou hast won the heights by humility, riches by poverty. Holy Father Nicholas, intercede with Christ our God that our souls may be saved.

FEAST DAY
January 17

Saint Anthony the Great

c. 245 – 350

BORN TO WEALTHY AND DEVOUT CHRISTIAN parents in Egypt, Anthony was always sensitive to the duties of faith. When his parents died, Anthony distributed his inheritance to the poor and went to live a life in solitude that set an example for centuries to come. Anthony is known as the Father of Monasticism, especially in the East.

Throughout his life, as Anthony removed himself from the pleasures and demands of the world, he was tempted and tormented by the devil. But Anthony kept himself strong through prayer and faith. Many were inspired by Anthony, and a community of disciples was built up around him, as in a monastery. St. Anthony died in 350, at the age of 105.

In his icon, St. Anthony's scroll contains words from one of his many writings: "I have seen in the snares of the devil." This also identifies the long spiritual warfare of the monastic with the devil, and his ultimate triumph. He is commemorated on January 17.

ST. ATHANASIUS

Saint Athanasius of Alexandria
295 – 373

A THANASIUS WAS BORN TO A CHRISTIAN family in Alexandria in 295. He was ordained the bishop of Alexandria before he reached his thirtieth birthday, and became a leader of the Church even before that.

At the time that Athanasius was serving the previous bishop, a local priest, Arius, spread the heresy that would be named for him. Arius claimed that Jesus Christ was not as divine as God Himself, and not the Son of God. Athanasius denounced Arianism immediately, and continued to denounce it as he was made bishop and throughout the rest of his life. Athanasius emphasized that the Incarnation is the beginning of salvation, that God became man, so that man can become like God. For some time, Athanasius struggled with the false accusations Arius' followers made against him, but he finally finished out his life in peace in Alexandria.

On St. Athanasius' scroll, the words "We give thanks to you, O Lord of Powers," call to mind the defense of Christ's divinity that he spent his life upholding.

FEAST DAY
January 18

FEAST DAY
January 28

Saint Ephrem the Syrian

c.306 – 375

ALTHOUGH HIS PARENTS WERE STRONG Christians, Ephrem, born in Nisbis, was thoughtless and rebellious in his youth. It was not until his antics bordered on crime and he was accused of theft that Ephrem began to repent of his ways, and he struggled for a while to truly repent, and not only fear punishment.

As a young man looking to change, Ephrem went into the wilderness to join a community of hermits. Under their guidance, he took to the life of a monk. He devoted himself to prayer, study, and writing. He composed hundreds of hymns, sermons, and apologetic works, and went on to teach outside his monastic community. St. Ephrem traveled for a period of his life and participated in the Church's development, but he spent his final years in a cave in silence and solitude. He is commemorated on January 28.

In the icon, St. Ephrem is dressed as a humble monk, showing his path in life, and holds a scroll, representing his many writings.

ST. BASIL

NO ONE BOUND UP BY WORLDLY DESIRES IS WORTH

BASIL WAS BORN IN CAESAREA IN 329, to a holy family full of saints. He went to complete his education in Athens, where he first met his lifelong friend St. Gregory the Theologian. Later, after he had spent some time in solitude, Basil became a priest back in Caesarea. He tirelessly wrote, studied, and served in Christ's name. But finally, from the weight of his many works, St. Basil died of exhaustion at the age of forty-nine.

St. Basil is known as the second of the three Great Hierarchs. Basil, his brother Gregory of Nyssa, and Gregory the Theologian were the great defenders of the divinity of Jesus Christ as well as our belief in the Holy Trinity.

One of St. Basil's greatest and most important works was his version of the Divine Liturgy. His icon portrays this. St. Basil and St. John Chrysostom, authors of the two main Liturgies whose texts are used in Orthodox churches today, are posed on either side of the altar. We use their words in the preparation of the Eucharist, so they are nearest the place where the Eucharist is prepared. The Divine Liturgy of St. Basil is celebrated ten times throughout the year, including on Sundays during Lent.

FEAST DAYS
January 1 and January 30

SAINT MELETIOS

FEAST DAY
February 12

Saint Meletios of Antioch † 381

MELETIOS, WHOSE NAME MAY ALSO appear as Meletius, is known as a great father of the Church. He was born in Armenia and lived an ascetic life from a young age. He was eventually ordained a bishop in Sebaste, in Turkey, but later came to be Archbishop of Antioch.

Meletios served as Archbishop during the fourth century, a time of great conflict in the Church. While not as outspoken as some defenders of the faith, Meletios still took a firm stance against heresy, and became a mentor to some of the Church Fathers who were to come after him. Having produced many writings on theology, Meletios died during the Second Ecumenical Council in 381. He is commemorated on February 12.

The icon of St. Meletios shows him in the vestments of a bishop, holding a gospel, as the Word whose truth he preached and promoted. His icon is located in the arch above the iconostas.

ST. GREGORY THE THEOLOGIAN

Saint Gregory the Theologian
329 – 389

GREGORY JOINED A LINE OF PROPHET and other holy men when his mothe promised him to God before he was born. H was born in 329, and his father, the bisho of Nazianzus, ordained him a priest in 36 Eleven years later he was ordained bishop o Sasima, and later became bishop of Constan tinople. He is now known as one of the thre Great Hierarchs, along with his lifelong frien Basil the Great and Gregory of Nyssa.

As a bishop, Gregory defended th Church's beliefs against the both the heresy of Arianism, which denied Jesus Christ's full and innate divinity, and the heresy of Apollinarian ism, which denied that He was as human as an other man. Gregory insisted that what Chris did not assume, was not healed.

St. Gregory's scroll reads, "You are hol and most holy, you and your only begotte son." This statement, taken from the Divin Liturgy of St. John Chrysostom, reaffirms Je sus' true nature.

Saint John Chrysostom

c. 349 – 407

S T. JOHN CHRYSOSTOM, BORN TWENTY or so years after St. Basil, was just as important in his legacy to the Church. When he completed his education, John began training as a monk. After a period of asceticism, he returned to Antioch, where he was ordained a priest and then a bishop. He would later become Patriarch of Constantinople.

As a Church leader living in civilization, John was active and eloquent. His name, *Chrysostom*, means *Golden Mouth*, and refers to the power of his preaching. He defended the theology and values of the Church in the face of powerful opponents. After offending the lavishly wealthy empress Eudoxia with his preaching, St. John was banished and died *en route* to Georgia. He is known as the third of the Great Hierarchs.

The writings of St. John Chrysostom are still widely read today. The text of his Divine Liturgy, somewhat shorter than St. Basil's, is the most common Liturgy used in the Orthodox Church. The words of his scroll, "O Lord our God, whose power is beyond compare," are from the liturgy of St. John Chrysostom, and refers to the divine mystery of the Eucharist, through which Christ becomes present in the Holy Gifts and is imparted to us.

FEAST DAYS
November 13, January 27, and January 30

IT IS TRULY PROPER TO GLORIFY YOU WHO HAVE BORN GOD

Saint Cyril of Alexandria
c. 376 – 444

CYRIL LIVED IN ALEXANDRIA IN THE fourth century. He succeeded his uncle, Theophilus, as Patriarch there.

Cyril is known for his defense against the heresy of Nestorius, the Patriarch of Constantinople. Nestorius claimed that while Jesus Christ was human and divine, His two natures were separate. With this claim, Nestorius also attacked Mary's role as *Theotokos*—the Mother of God—because as an earthly woman she could only give birth to Jesus' human nature. To Nestorius, Mary was only *Christotokos*—the Mother of Christ. Cyril held that, because Jesus is indivisibly divine and human, Mary can be nothing but the Mother of God, for Mary gave birth to a Person, not a "nature."

Much of St. Cyril's life was taken up in his defense of Mary as Theotokos, but he also wrote many valuable Epistles. He fell asleep in the Lord in 444.

The icon of St. Cyril reveals his defense of the Theotokos. He is shown looking up in adoration at the *Platytera* icon (p. 66), and holding a scroll which reads, "It is truly proper to glorify you who have born God," a brief and full declaration of the truth.

FEAST DAYS

FEAST DAY
March 14

Saint Benedict of Nursia

480 – 547

IN 480, BENEDICT WAS BORN IN NURSIA, a city in Italy. While he was in his teens, he was sent to Rome to finish his secular education. But once he was there, Benedict decided to devote himself to a religious life.

Known as the father of Western Monasticism, Benedict lived his life as an example for monastics to come. Many came to hear his teachings and to live as he did, in simplicity and devotion to God. Soon Benedict had so many followers that he divided them into communities, and founded a monastic order based on adherence to his "Rule" which established their way of life. For a long while the Benedictine Order, with its focus on scholarship, work, and self-sacrifice, was the dominant form of monasticism in the West.

St. Benedict reposed in 547. He is commemorated on March 14.

In his icon, Benedict's scroll reads "*Ora et Labora,*" Latin for "Pray and Work," the law he lived for himself and taught generations of others to live for as well.

FEAST DAY
October 1

Saint Romanos the Melodist

c. 490 – 556

ROMANOS WAS BORN IN EDESSA, IN SYRia, in the fifth century. He was involved in the Church from a young age. After serving as a deacon in Beirut, he went on to Constantinople. Romanos remained a passionate servant of the Church, but felt that his voice was not strong enough to fully sing God's praise. Traditionally, the Theotokos herself made Romanos' voice strong.

After this, Romanos was inspired to write a *Kontakion*, or hymn of praise, for the Nativity. He then wrote a wealth of songs for feasts and saints. Romanos' legacy, the hymns, music, and poetry he composed, is very much alive and known in the Orthodox Church.

The Greek word *Kontakion* refers to the stick around which a scroll was wrapped. Romanos in the icon holds a scroll with words from one of his *Kontakia*. He wears a deacon's vestments, and carries the Gospel book a deacon carries and reads in an Orthodox liturgy. It is the same Gospel Romanos glorified with his music.

FEAST DAYS
April 1 and the fifth Sunday of Great Lent

Saint Mary of Egypt

† 5th or 6th century

AS A YOUNG GIRL IN THE FIFTH CENTURY, Mary left home for Egypt's capital city, Alexandria. There she enjoyed a luxuriously sinful life in her youth, until she joined a group of pilgrims heading for Jerusalem. Mary had no interest in the religious side of the journey, but joined for pleasure and adventure.

In Jerusalem, Mary tried to enter the Church of the Resurrection with rest of her group, but an invisible force came up against her and would not let her inside. This sign drove to Mary to prayer and repentance. She retired into the wilderness as an ascetic, remained in solitude for decades, and reposed shortly after giving her testimony to the monk St. Zosimas.

St. Mary is commemorated on April 1 and also on the fifth Sunday of Great Lent.

The icon of St. Mary of Egypt shows her as she was near the end of her years of repentance. She is portrayed as an old, weathered woman in the rough robe of an ascetic, holding the Cross to which she devoted her life.

ST. GREGORY THE DIALOGUS

O LORD, BLESS THOSE WHO PRAISE YOU

Saint Gregory Dialogus
c. 540 – 604

A**LSO KNOWN AS** S**T.** G**REGORY OF** R**OME,** Gregory Dialogus is the Church Father shown in our icons who played the greatest role in developing Western Christianity.

Gregory was born to a wealthy family in Rome in 540, and was brought up to become a Roman official. He gave up his wealth and position, though, and devoted his life to God. He converted his own home into a monastery. He was ordained as a deacon in the Roman Church, and eventually became the Pope of Rome.

As Pope, Gregory re-energized missionary work in Northern Europe and the Church spread. He played a major role in the conversion of England. He also wrote his *Dialogues*, a discussion of his views on Christianity. (It is from that title that St. Gregory gets the name *Dialogus*.) He is credited with writing the Divine Liturgy of the Presanctified Gifts, which is served in many Orthodox churches during Great Lent.

St. Gregory died a natural death in Rome in 604, and was immediately recognized as a saint.

In the icon, St. Gregory's scroll contains a line from both his *Dialogues* and a prayer from the Liturgy: "O Lord bless those who praise you."

Saint Andrew of Crete

c. 650 – 740

ANDREW WAS ALSO BORN IN DAMASCUS in the seventh century, but is known for becoming the bishop of Crete later in his life. He began his time in the church as a monk in Jerusalem when he was in his teens, and for his wisdom and dedication was promoted up the hierarchy of clergy.

Not only is Andrew known for being in attendance at the Sixth Ecumenical Council and there defending Church teachings against heresy, but also for the hymns and works of praise he wrote. St. Andrew is responsible for a kind of hymn, composed of many verses, called a *canon. The Canon of St. Andrew* is traditionally read at the beginning of Great Lent.

St. Andrew died a natural death while traveling back to Crete in the early eighth century. He is commemorated on July 4.

Like other Church fathers, St. Andrew is vested as a bishop in his icon. He holds the Gospel, and opens his arms in praise while making the Byzantine blessing.

SAINT DAMA~ JOHN ~SCENE

WHICH ODE IS WORTHY TO PRAISE YOU

FEAST DAY
December 4

Saint John Damascene

c. 676 – 749

JOHN DAMASCENE, WHOSE NAME MEANS "of Damascus," was born in Damascus, Syria, in the seventh century. He grew up to be an outspoken defender of iconography.

Despite a warning from Byzantine Emperor Leo III, John continued to write in defense of icons. The emperor tricked the ruling caliph in Damascus into cutting off John's hand. Because this was the hand John wrote with, he keenly felt the loss. After much prayer, and a promise to write praise for the Orthodox Church, John had a vision of the Theotokos, who restored his hand. John spent the rest of his life writing hymns and prayers (many of which are still used today), and lived until the age of 104. He is commemorated on December 4.

The icon of St. John shows him dressed in the manner of an Arab culture. A line from one of his hymns of praise is on his scroll, and a red scar, from the healing, is visible on his right wrist.

Saint Irene Chrysovalantou

† 9th century

THE DAUGHTER OF ARISTOCRATS IN Cappdocia, Irene was chosen to marry the son of the Byzantine Empress. But while on her way to the wedding, Irene was inspired to become a sister at the humble monastery of Chrysovalantou.

Irene gave up her wealth and inheritance to people in need and performed the most menial tasks with joy. Even as she was made abbess of the monastery, she led an ascetic life within the community, and was granted the gifts to per-form miracles and signs for the glory of God.

After reaching the age of one hundred, Irene foresaw her own death, and spent days in prayer for preparation. When she reposed, in the middle of the ninth century, Irene's body gave off a sweet fragrance, her last sign from God. St. Irene is commemorated on July 28.

In the icon, St. Irene holds both a cross, representing her devotion, and a pair of apples, representing one of the signs she performed during her life.

SAINC PALA~

GREGORY ~MAS

FEAST DAYS
November 14 and the second Sunday of Great Lent

Saint Gregory Palamas

1296 – 1359

GREGORY WAS BORN IN CONSTANTINO-ple in the fourteenth century. He and his brothers joined a monastery on Mount Athos.

Gregory is remembered for his defense of *Hesychasm* in the fourteenth century. The Hesychasts sought a mystical vision of the Divine Light through a rigorous life of prayer. Such practice went counter to the prevailing idea, especially in the West, that God was unknowable through human experience. By distinguishing the experience of God's *energies* from His *essence*, Gregory defended the Hesychasts against Barlaam the Calabrian and others, and affirmed that we can seek an immediate relationship with God who is Light, while preserving God's ultimate transcendence.

St. Gregory reposed in 1359, after serving as Archbishop of Thessalonica.

In his icon, St. Gregory's hair and beard reflect his role as a monastic, but he is also vested as a bishop. He holds the Gospel book and gives his blessing.

SAINT MARK OF EPHESUS

FEAST DAY
January 19

Saint Mark of Ephesus

1392 – 1444

A DEFENDER OF THE ORTHODOX FAITH after the Great Schism with the Church of Rome, Mark was born at the end of the fourteenth century. As the Archbishop of Ephesus, he was especially outspoken at the Council of Florence in Italy in 1439.

At the council, Mark presented his defense of several key points that marked the distinction between the Orthodox faith and developments in the Western church. He is known for holding to the Orthodox version of the Creed after the Western addition of the word *filioque*, which means the Holy Spirit proceeds from both the Father and the Son. Mark stood alone, also being the only Eastern bishop at the council who refused to acknowledge the universal authority of the Western Church and the Pope of Rome.

St. Mark died from an illness at the age of fifty-two. He is commemorated on January 19.

The icon of St. Mark shows him as another Church Father, as a bishop holding the Gospel book and giving a blessing.

Saint Seraphim of Sarov

1759 – 1833

ORIGINALLY CALLED PROKHOR, ST. SERaphim was born to middle-class parents in Russia in 1754. He became very ill as a young child, but was healed by the wonderworking Kursk Root Icon through his own faith and the faith of his mother. After this experience, he dedicated himself the Church, and at the age of eighteen set himself to be a monk.

In the monastery, where he was named Seraphim, the saint ate and slept very little, devoting all his focus to prayer. He was again miraculously healed of illness, and saw and made many signs and wonders. As he grew older, Seraphim withdrew from the monastery and went into the wilderness. He achieved great wisdom in his contemplation, and many people sought his advice and encouragement. Seraphim died in 1833, and is commemorated on January 2.

St. Seraphim appears as a humble Russian monk in his icon, holding a strand of prayer rope. His time and place, and his form of devotion, are all represented.

FEAST DAYS
October 6 and March 31

Saint Innocent of Alaska   *1797 – 1879*

Born John Veniaminov in Irkutsk in 1797, Innocent was educated in the beliefs of the church from a young age. He entered seminary once he was old enough, and married before he was ordained a deacon and then a priest.

In 1823, he was called to serve as a missionary and educator in the nearby Aleutian Islands. For years, on the Aleutian Islands and later on the island of Sitka, Innocent and his family devoted themselves to bringing the native peoples to Christ. Also known as the "Apostle to America," Innocent, who took his new name after his wife died and he became a bishop in Russia, died himself in 1879, while serving as Metropolitan of Moscow. He is commemorated on both October 6 and March 31.

In the icon, St. Innocent, giving a blessing, has the vestments and staff of his time and place. His placement above our iconostas reminds us that he was responsible, originally, for Orthodoxy's presence in North America.

Saint Alexis Toth of Wilkes-Barre   *1853 – 1909*

THE SON OF A PRIEST IN HUNGARY, Alexis was born in 1854. After receiving a Roman Catholic education, he married and was ordained a priest in the Greek Catholic Uniate church, a church of Orthodox tradition under Catholic authority. After his wife's early death, Alexis was appointed to serve in Minneapolis.

Once there, Alexis found that the bishop would not acknowledge him as a Catholic priest, and that his own Uniate parish would be stronger if it returned to the Orthodox Church. Alexis worked tirelessly throughout his life to educate and support Uniate communities in the United States as they returned to the Orthodox Church. His writings preached tolerance of other beliefs, but also presented Orthodox doctrine in a way understandable to newcomers.

St. Alexis died in Pennsylvania in 1909.

In the icon, St. Alexis is vested as a priest. His book reads, "This is the faith of the Apostles, this is the faith of our Fathers," from the proclamation used for the Triumph of Orthodoxy, and showing his lifelong dedication to Orthodoxy as the true faith.

Saint Raphael of Brooklyn

1860 – 1915

R APHAEL OF BROOKLYN, OR RAPHAEL Hawaweeny, was born in Beirut in 1860. He spent the first few decades of his life in various parts of the Middle East and Russia, immigrating with changing political tides, being educated and rising in the Orthodox clergy.

Raphael was called to the United States and established a parish Brooklyn. He served several small communities of Orthodox immigrants, encouraging them to keep practicing their faith. After becoming Bishop of Brooklyn and the first Orthodox bishop consecrated in America, Raphael traveled the world giving the same encouragement and strength to similar communities who had no other Church authority nearby.

St. Raphael reposed in 1915. During his life he visited Grand Rapids and the community that founded St. Nicholas at least twice.

Photographs of St. Raphael do exist, and so we know his icons are close likenesses. St. Raphael's vestments are simpler and more modern than those of the older Church Fathers, and he holds the Gospel that he spread and supported throughout North America.

Saint Tikhon the Confessor

1865 – 1925

S T. TIKHON WAS BORN VASSILY BELAVIN in Pskov, Russia, in 1865. His father was an Orthodox priest, and he set himself early on to follow the same calling. He attended seminary in St. Petersburg, and took the name Tikhon when he became a monk.

Tikhon went to spread and uphold Orthodoxy throughout the world. As the first Orthodox bishop to be present in North America, he founded the first Orthodox seminary in the United States and promoted the use of English in American Orthodoxy. Later he was made Patriarch of Moscow and All Russia. As the rise of the Bolsheviks made Russia an atheist state, he continued in his duties as an Orthodox pastor. St. Tikhon either died naturally or was martyred in a hospital in Russia in 1925.

In his icon, St. Tikhon wears the traditional white mitre of the Patriarch of Moscow. He makes a blessing with one hand, and holds a candle with the other. Tikhon's candle reflects his role as "the Enlightener of North America," as he is sometimes known, lighting the path of Orthodoxy to those in the New World.

SAINT OF JOHN SHANGHAI

Saint John of Shanghai

1895 – 1966

BORN MICHAEL MAXIMOVICH IN THE Ukraine IN 1895, John attended law school, and then went on to seminary. By then, the anti-religious Bolsheviks were fully in power, and so he became a monk in Serbia, where he took the name John. He was ordained a priest shortly afterward.

As a Russian priest in exile, John served in Shanghai, China, where he established many institutions for the people's benefit. When his work there was finished, John was assigned to Paris. There he worked to revive the veneration of Western saints who were forgotten in the Schism.

In 1962 he was made Archbishop of San Francisco. It was there that he was revealed as a wonderworker. For a long while John served his diocese with childlike joy and patience, sometimes miraculously healing parishioners and giving signs.

Exhausted by a parish conflict, St. John fell asleep in the Lord in Seattle in 1966.

St. John's garments in his icons are reminiscent of his role as a bishop. He holds his hand in blessing.

The presence of this icon of St. John, who was only glorified in 1994, reminds us that the joy, purpose, and miracles of the ancient Church are very much alive today. In fact, our iconographer, Fr. Koufous, once met St. John.

The last icon to describe, the image on the iconostasis of Our Lord, God, and Savior Jesus Christ returning in glory, reminds us that the love on which the Church was founded has been and will remain alive forever.

Epilogue

BY PHOTOGRAPHER
DAVID J. DEJONGE

THE TEN-FOOT DOORS WERE LODGED OPEN and a dusty haze filled the air, illuminated by the light filtering through the windows. In the center of the church was a stairwell that zigzagged vertically and disappeared into the hazed top of the structure. Chipped and seasoned yellow scaffolding ascended as far as the eye could see. A plywood platform rested upon the top of the steel structure, forming a canvas, shielding the top from below.

After 20 years as a photographer and a lifetime of Christian teaching, my life was about to change. I call this moment "the scaffold of divine ascent." I approached the stairs and looked up and behind me. I quietly said to myself one of my life sayings, "A journey of a thousand miles begins with one step." And so, this journey began as I stepped onto the stairs.

This was an intriguing assignment one that was steeped in mystery both in my life and that of the construction around me in this church. As I began the slow ascent I was astounded at how much the entire manmade structure shifted with my every step. It was this movement that let those working above immediately know someone new was arriving.

The soft voices echoing above, muted by the wood separating us, announced there was a new person coming up. Step by step I climbed to find myself at the top of the scaffold. I could no longer see what was happening below; I could only see those things surrounding me, 70 feet above the floor. The workers were actively working on the dome of St. Nicholas Antiochian Orthodox Church in Grand Rapids, Michigan.

At the top of the steps I was greeted by not only artists, but also expert Church historians actively working at their artistry—if it can be called artistry. More than nice pictures to look at, it was a profound lesson on deeper levels. Is it about the iconography itself, or about the journey of those who see it?

What happens when you take a lifelong Protestant Christian and drop him into a world of iconography representing 2000 years of Church history? For me, it was a transformation and a desire to share the journey and knowledge with others.

As a Protestant, there was always a mystery as to how the Christian faith became what it is today. For many, the Christian history seemed to go from the death and resurrection of Jesus Christ and skip directly to 1517 and Martin Luther. And with Martin Luther and the Reformation an invisible shield of Christian history exists, blocking the founding Fathers of Christianity and leading many to speculate on foundations that have been well-known and understood since the beginning. Were there original instructions on baptism of infants or adults? And what of worship? How did the early Christians practice their faith?

Everything in the Orthodox Christian faith is systematically done, systematically linked, and like clockwork; structured, methodical, and ordered. Like the scaffold on which I stood, the wisdom of the Church Fathers was critical to the stability and the future of the Church. The early Church miraculously set in place a series of checks and balances to assure consistency, accuracy, and critical layers of protection that would endure the test of time. Yet the Church is a divine *and* human organism, and is not without human scandal and issue. As Fr. Daniel Daly told me, "The Orthodox Christian faith is filled with humans that fail, but the theology will always remain the same. You can have your own opinion but you can't have your own facts."

In this assignment I discovered the 1500 missing years of how Christianity was chiseled, shaped and forged. This was a vast discovery of the blood—not only the Blood of my Lord, but

also the blood of those who forged our Faith, and the blood of those willing to give all to faithfully share the Good News of forgiveness and love: daughters killed by fathers for their love for Christ, and miracles never before heard.

In five years of studying Church history and iconography, I have found that everything within the Orthodox Christian faith is chain-linked together to the past. *Orthodoxy* is defined as *correct* or *right praise*. But by what rules can orthodoxy be defined? No person or denomination can declare himself or herself Orthodox, for there must first be a set of defining beliefs, rules, and structure.

Much like the manmade structure of scaffolding that was built to construct this temple, eventually the men who made the structure and icons will fade away. The manmade structures can be flawed, damaged, and imperfect. For those within the profession of iconography, there is no room for imperfection, as these images are visual stories to indicate to people today and in the future of the faith and outside of it the story of Christianity.

Again, like the structure of the scaffolds, the iconography is symbolic and historic, and must adhere to centuries of consistency and instruction. Iconography has been called "theology in color." I, as a mere human working to capture the photographs of this book, will fade away as well. And when the men and women fade away, what remains will chain-link to the future so others as well can trust the foundation described within this book. If we have done our jobs properly you will look at the images rather than us. The history depicted within the iconography and photographs should be able to tell the story of Christianity completely and accurately.

For the purposes of this book, we have specifically chosen to not delve into the theological aspects of veneration, worship, and prayer using iconography. If this perplexes you, we invite you to investigate and examine Church history using the full spectrum of study now available, or seek the counsel of an Orthodox priest. These topics, however, were scrutinized by the Christian Church and set in stone at the Seventh Ecumenical Council in 787 AD.

I have done thousands of hours of study in preparation of this book and found many surprises about my own beliefs. Some, which I had thought were Biblical, have turned out to be chain-linked to history and teachings that were in error. When I followed those rabbit trails to their end, I was perplexed and challenged. Nevertheless, a good study of Church

history will yield clarity by contrast for those who are curious, and will ultimately help clarify your own beliefs, wherever you may end up.

The preparation of this book was taken with the utmost seriousness in order to "hold fast to the traditions [we] have been taught" (2 Th. 2:15). For those unfamiliar with Orthodox Christianity, and the Antiochian Church in particular, it is the very same Church that was founded by the Apostle Peter in Antioch, thus the term *Antiochian*. The Orthodox Christian faith also gave the world the creeds that many still profess, or use as a basis for denominations outside of the Orthodox Churches.

Orthodox Christianity teaches *Apostolic Succession*, the belief that teachings of the Apostles, and the authority to teach, is passed down from the Apostles through ages. This book will introduce you to some of those who are a part of that 2000-year line of succession.

As a lifelong historian and photojournalist, my training has always been to get as close to the source of the story as I could. That has always meant going to the witnesses to gather information. What was ultimately found in this project was "a great cloud of witnesses" to Christian history, in the form of icons, theologians, and priests. Hopefully, to find the witnesses is to find the truth. From there one can truly assess and determine our own beliefs.

The scaffolding at St. Nicholas has long been taken apart, removed, replaced with humans to share this faith with the world allowing those below to fully view those above. For now, each person in a pew stands to support the faith, the history, the reputation of what Christianity is.

With the removal of the scaffolding, we can see the icons clearly. Those in the next world are witnessing clearly how men and women have assembled and disassembled their own lives—each person's own "scaffold of divine ascent." What are the pieces in our own lives that need repair? What acts of mercy are we not tending to? Are we spreading the news about truth that could bring peace? What poor are we ignoring? What hurting need to be helped? Have we given up the first class seat to clothe the poor and the homeless? Do we help our neighbors the way we would help strangers on a mission trip overseas? What spiritually lost need help?

Consider the icons and what they point to. Perhaps those men and women *beyond the image*, who have completed their race, are watching our lives the entire time to see whether we, like them, are working to become like God.

Let mercy lead us.

A Timeline of Church History

IN THE ICONS OF SAINT NICHOLAS CHURCH

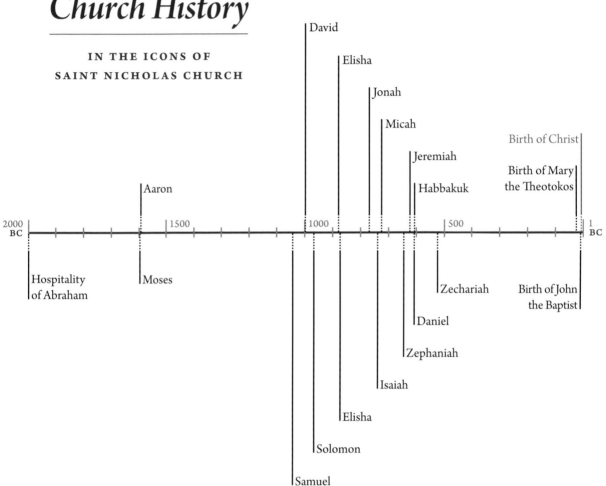

David

Elisha

Jonah

Micah

Jeremiah

Birth of Christ

Habbakuk

Birth of Mary
the Theotokos

Aaron

2000
BC

1500

1000

500

1
BC

Hospitality
of Abraham

Moses

Zechariah

Birth of John
the Baptist

Daniel

Zephaniah

Isaiah

Elisha

Solomon

Samuel

Patriarchs	Exodus	Judges	United Kingdom	Divided Kingdom	Babylonian Exile	Fall to Greeks	Fall to Romans
	Egyptian Slavery	Conquest of Canaan		Prophets		Restoration	Maccabees & Hasmoneans

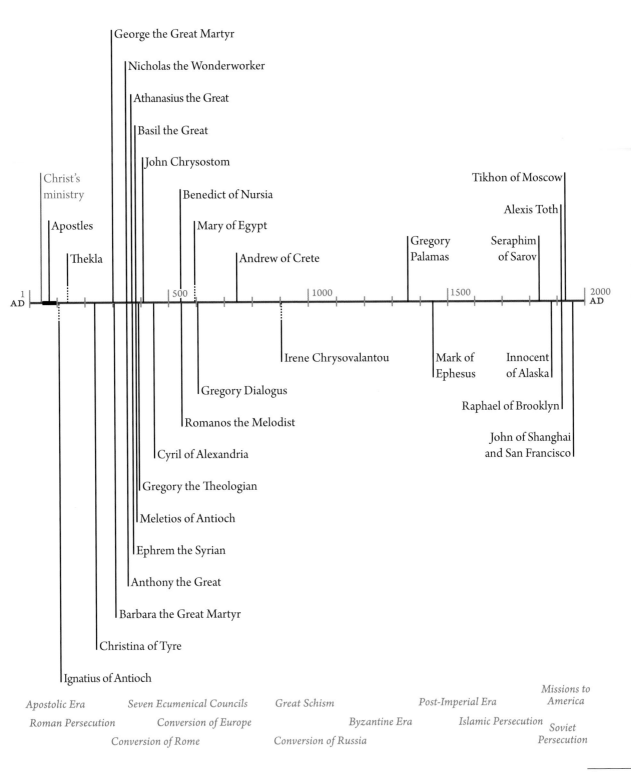

George the Great Martyr

Nicholas the Wonderworker

Athanasius the Great

Basil the Great

John Chrysostom

Benedict of Nursia

Mary of Egypt

Christ's ministry

Apostles

Thekla

Andrew of Crete

Tikhon of Moscow

Alexis Toth

Gregory Palamas

Seraphim of Sarov

1 AD

500

1000

1500

2000 AD

Irene Chrysovalantou

Mark of Ephesus

Innocent of Alaska

Gregory Dialogus

Romanos the Melodist

Cyril of Alexandria

Raphael of Brooklyn

John of Shanghai and San Francisco

Gregory the Theologian

Meletios of Antioch

Ephrem the Syrian

Anthony the Great

Barbara the Great Martyr

Christina of Tyre

Ignatius of Antioch

Apostolic Era

Seven Ecumenical Councils

Great Schism

Post-Imperial Era

Missions to America

Roman Persecution

Conversion of Europe

Byzantine Era

Islamic Persecution

Soviet Persecution

Conversion of Rome

Conversion of Russia

Bibliography

Bouteneff, Peter. *Sweeter than Honey: Orthodox Thinking on Dogma and Truth*. Crestwood, NY: St. Vladimir's Seminary Press, 2006. Print.

Bunge, Gabriel. *The Rublev Trinity*. Crestwood, NY: St. Vladimir's Seminary Press, 2007. Print.

"Calendar for Feasts, Fasts, and Commemorations." *The Self-Ruled Antiochian Christian Archdiocese of America*. Antiochian Archdiocese, Web. 16 Mar 2011. <http://www.antiochian.org/calendar>

"Category: 'Saints.'" *Orthodoxwiki*. Web. 16 Mar 2011. <http://orthodoxwiki.org/Category:Saints>.

Koufus, Theodore. Telephone Interview by Katherine Khorey. July 15, 2010. 16 Mar 2011.

"Lives of the Saints, The." *Orthodox Church of America*. OCA, Web. 16 Mar 2011. <http://www.oca.org/fslives.asp>.

Lossky, Vladimir, and Leonid Ouspensky. *The Meaning of Icons*. Crestwood, NY: St. Vladimir's Seminary Press, 1983. Print.

Najim, V. Rev. Fr. Michel, trans. "St. Joseph of Damascus." *St. John of Damascus Institute of Theology, Balamand University*. N.p., n.d. Web. 16 Mar 2011. <http://www.balamand.edu.lb/theology/SaintJosephDamascus.htm>. (Reprinted from *Word Magazine*, Jan. 1994, pp. 21-26)

Quenot, Michel. *The Icon: Window on the Kingdom*. Crestwood, NY: St. Vladimir's Seminary Press, 1991. Print.

Ware, Timothy. *The Orthodox Church*. 1964. Print.

☦   ☦   ☦

Abbreviations of the Books of the Bible

Ge	Genesis	Job	Job	Mt	Matthew
Ex	Exodus	Pr	Proverbs of Solomon	Mk	Mark
Le	Leviticus	Ec	Ecclesiastes	Lk	Luke
Nu	Numbers	CC	Canticle of Canticles (= Song of Songs)	Jn	John
De	Deuteronomy			Ac	Acts
Jos	Joshua	Wi	Wisdom of Solomon	Ro	Romans
Jdg	Judges	Si	Wisdom of Sirach (= Ecclesiasticus)	1Cor	1 Corinthians
Ru	Ruth			2Cor	2 Corinthians
1Kgd	1 Kingdoms (= 1 Samuel)	Ho	Hosea	Ga	Galatians
		Am	Amos	Eph	Ephesians
2Kgd	2 Kingdoms (= 2 Samuel)	Mi	Micah	Php	Philippians
		Jl	Joel	Col	Colossians
3Kgd	3 Kingdoms (= 1 Kings)	Ob	Obadiah	1Th	1 Thessalonians
		Jon	Jonah	2Th	2 Thessalonians
4Kgd	4 Kingdoms (= 2 Kings)	Na	Nahum	1Ti	1 Timothy
		Hb	Habakkuk	2Ti	2 Timothy
1Pa	1 Paralipomenon (= 1 Chronicles)	Zph	Zephaniah	Ti	Titus
		Hg	Haggai	Phl	Philemon
2Pa	2 Paralipomenon (= 2 Chronicles)	Zc	Zechariah	He	Hebrews
		Ml	Malachi	Ja	James
1Esd	1 Esdras	Is	Isaiah	1Pe	1 Peter
2Esd	2 Esdras (= Ezra or Ezra-Nehemiah)	Je	Jeremiah	2Pe	2 Peter
		EJ	Epistle of Jeremiah	1Jn	1 John
Ne	Nehemiah	La	Lamentations	2Jn	2 John
To	Tobit	Ez	Ezekiel	3Jn	3 John
Jth	Judith	Da	Daniel (incl. Susanna, Song of the Three Youths, and Bel)	Ju	Jude
Es	Esther			Re	Revelation (= Apocalypse of John)
1Ma	1 Maccabees				
2Ma	2 Maccabees				
3Ma	3 Maccabees				
Ps	Psalms*				

O.T. APPENDIX†

4Ma	4 Maccabees
3Esd	3 Esdras (= Apocalypse of Ezra)

* There are 151 Psalms, and the Greek numbering differs from the Hebrew.

† The acceptance of these books varies throughout the Orthodox Church.

"GLORY TO GOD FOR ALL THINGS."

—St. John Chrysostom